WESKER'S MONOLOGUES

Arnold Wesker's
MONOLOGUES

142 speeches for actors – professional, training
or amateur – for students of theatre,
and for anyone who loves the spoken word

OBERON BOOKS
LONDON

First published in 2008 by Oberon Books Ltd
521 Caledonian Road, London N7 9RH
Tel: 020 7607 3637 / Fax: 020 7607 3629
email: info@oberonbooks.com
www.oberonbooks.com

Monologues from *Chicken Soup with Barley, Roots, I'm Talking about Jerusalem* and *Shylock* reproduced with kind permission of Methuen Drama. (Methuen Drama publishes *Shylock* as *The Merchant*.)

Monolgues from *Longitude* reproduced with kind permission of Amber Lane Press.

A catalogue record for this book is available from the British Library.

Cover photograph by Nobby Clark

ISBN 978-1-84002-792-1

Printed in Great Britain by Antony Rowe, Chippenham

Contents

In memory of my dear friend
Yildiz Arda OBE

Preface

Most writers are surprised by the amount they have written in a lifetime. I am amazed to have combed 44 of my plays and revealed 68 different characters offering 142 monologues – 41 for men, 27 for women. Not included are any of the cycle of *One Woman Plays* for 11 female characters, printed in Volume 2 of two volumes published by Methuen Books. (Volume 1 is The Wesker Trilogy consisting of *Chicken Soup With Barley, Roots, I'm Talking About Jerusalem.*) Together with this volume, Oberon Books have published a volume entitled 'Wesker's Love Plays' consisting of *The Four Seasons, Love Letters on Blue Paper* and *Lady Othello.* Other out of print volumes are available on the internet at www.abebooks.co.uk.

The main intention of this anthology is to offer actors and students of drama a range of audition pieces; but it is also hoped that the collection will introduce a public to the later plays, which may not be as familiar as the earlier ones.

The frozen image is the curse of the artist. 'Retrospectives' help, but whereas retrospectives are economically viable for the film director, painter or sculptor they are impossible for the playwright. A collection such as contained in this volume is the nearest we can get. If I have a discernable 'voice' it will emerge through the material of these speeches rather than what's thought of as 'style'.

I worry about writers who straightjacket their material into personal mannerisms which are confused as their 'voice', their 'style', rather than allowing material to dictate its own inherent style. I believe a writer's 'voice' is identified not by an instantly recognisable trick of dialogue but by the way their intelligence and sensitivity perceive and record their experience of life.

This assembly of speeches, then, is also a shorthand way of sharing those perceptions as well as being a 'retrospective'.

I've slightly altered the beginning of some speeches, taking from the previous speech those words without which there would be no intelligible lead-in; others have been strung together with dots... indicating that another character's lines have been omitted. In this way each speech has a life of its own. A brief synopsis of the play helps place it in its context.

The canvas of theme and emotion contained within these speeches is, hopefully, rich and varied enough to meet the needs of very diverse performers.

Themes: friendship, dying, old age, political disillusion, failed love, achieved love, self-discovery...

Emotions: anger, joy, hope, fear, outrage, love, humour, bewilderment, guilt, comic irony...

I hereby offer...

Arnold Wesker

25 February 2008

INDEX
plays, characters, first lines

couldn't focus on anything. He kept shouting in Yiddish, calling for his mothee… **43**

ESTHER My mother loved her children. You know how I know? The way she used to cook our food. With songs. She used to hum and feed us. Sing and dress us. Coo and scold us. **44**

DAVE What do you think I am, Ronnie? You think I'm an artist's craftsman? Nothing of the sort. A designer? Not even that. Designers are ten a penny. I don't mind Ronnie – believe me… **45**

CHIPS WITH EVERYTHING (1962)

CORPORAL HILL That's better. In future, whenever an NCO comes into the hut, no matter who he is, the first person to see him will call out 'NCO! NCO!' Like that. **47**

PIP Look old son, you're going to have me for eight painful weeks in the same hut, so spend the next five minutes taking the mickey out of my accent, get it off your chest and then put your working-class halo away because no one's going to care. **49**

PILOT OFFICER It goes right through us, Thompson. Nothing you can do will change that. We listen but we do not hear, we befriend but do not touch you, we applaud but do not act – to tolerate is to ignore. **51**

SMILER LEAVE ME ALONE! Damn your mouths and hell on your stripes – leave me alone. Mad they are, they're mad they are, they're raving lunatics they are. **52**

THE FOUR SEASONS (1965)

BEATRICE I can't, I can't, that's it. I can't. No sound, I make no sounds, just a long moan, or a silence. I destroyed a marriage and failed a lover, now leave me alone, damn you. Leave me alone… I just can't sing… **54**

ADAM Two kinds of love, two kinds of women. The woman whose love embraces you, the woman whose love oppresses you. The first keeps its distance, and you

THE OLD ONES (1970)

Three speeches of Teressa

The third of three confrontational speeches from Rosa

whisper, whisper, pssssss! Why don't they ask me? Ask me, I'll tell them…

LOVE LETTERS ON BLUE PAPER (1976)

Five speeches of Victor

Sonia's eight love letters

SHYLOCK (PREVIOUSLY *THE MERCHANT* 1976)

ONE MORE RIDE ON THE MERRY-GO-ROUND (1978)

WHEN GOD WANTED A SON (1976)

Two Cabaret appearances by Connie

LADY OTHELLO (1987)

BLUEY (1993)

Four speeches from Leo

BLOOD LIBEL (1991)

WILD SPRING (1992)

GERTIE Well. What do I say? I know – that's what everyone asks: 'what do I say?' and then everyone thanks everyone. And I do. Everyone. Thank them… Oh dear – you can tell I didn't expect to win, I'm not prepared. **200**

GERTIE Well mums are always a good standby for off-loading blame. Problem with my mum was she taught me to blame myself. For everything. **201**

GERTIE When I close my eyes I can see Palmers Green. The tiny, dreary, two-up two-down behind the curtains of which, wrote the poet, are people living out their lives of quiet desperation. **202**

SAM When I close my eyes – hills. Purple hills. Behind me. In front – a beach. All sand. No stones. No stones and no people. **203**

GERTIE I'm sorry, Tom. Some things I could do for you, some I couldn't. Some things I can help, some I can't. **205**

GERTIE You thought that was my best so far, did you? Yes, well I'm feeling a little sad today, perhaps that helps. (*Listens.*) Oh, nothing serious. Just one of those days. It'll pass. **206**

GERTIE …Can you tremble like that?… You think I am just acting. 'Just acting'. Are you aware, Mr Phillips, that society normally uses the name of our profession as a term of abuse? 'Oh ignore her, she's just acting!' **208**

KENNEDY My mum? Married at seventeen, had five children, and when the youngest was fourteen said goodbye to us all and went off with a dark stranger. **210**

KENNEDY It so happens I'm good with money… I actually do understand money… I'll confess something – I've actually made money. **211**

GERTIE Ah, food. Now, if you really want to know and understand everything about me, and you *do* want to know and understand everything about me don't you, Mr Phillips, because that's the only way you'll get me into bed… **212**

GERTIE You want to be an actor, Kennedy, but could you cope with rejection? That's the killer. Coping with

MATTY 'Twenty fifth of October nineteen ninety-nine. Oh, Mark. I can't sleep, I can't read, I can't sit still, I can't stop thinking about everything you said. Everything *I* said! You made me surprise myself. **231**

LONGITUDE (2002)

HARRISON What were it about me? They called me 'strange'. Strange? What were there strange? I made clocks. Taught myself to make clocks, what were strange about that? **233**

HARRISON And then – along comes a ticking thing in a box invented not by a priest or professor but by an uneducated carpenter. A ticking thing in a box! Ha! A clock! Oh my goodness deary me. Tick tock tick tock! A clock! Oh deary deary me. **234**

HARRISON Then, sir, it's about time you did hear talk like that, for if this goes on…if you prevaricate…more ships will wreck themselves upon rocks and more women and children will be made widows and orphans… **235**

HARRISON I'm a thorn in their side. Nothing will please them but my death. Well die I won't. I'll hell not die. I know all about them as glory in the end of things, the passing of this and that. *He's* had his day, they say with sadness in their voice and glee in their dried up hearts. **236**

PHOENIX PHOENIX BURNING BRIGHT (2006)

JANIKA I have this dread of something awful about to happen. It's not a fear of the bomb, I don't think it's that, but some kind of anarchy. A break-up of patterns of behaviour. **238**

RAPHAEL Awful man! Loud mouthed, patronising, a kind of hearty bully. I once saw him, after the News. There'd been a competition and the prize was an opportunity to run around a supermarket with a trolley and pack as much into it as you could in three minutes. **239**

KARL-OLAF This! This poor girl. What they did to her. Couldn't sleep. **240**

JANIKA Oh, it's not interesting. Boring old blue-stocking stuff. We all have complaints. But endless long monologues of complaint become a habit. **241**

THE ROCKING HORSE (2007)

CLARA You're still lonely, Clara. You've created rituals for yourself but you're still lonely. I sit here in my garden, Clara's garden, and I realise how much I love life, but it doesn't stop me feeling lonely, just lonely, lonely. **243**

AGNES I'm Agnes and I shall never forget. It will remain with me always. We were in a restaurant. Very expensive. He wanted to buy me a special meal for a 'special occasion' he said. **244**

RAMBO Yeah! My family actually did christen me Rambo. Don't much look like him though. Don't think I much *want* to look like him, either. All them muscles – too heavy to carry around, man. **245**

MARVIN My son was killed here. Just there, where Cazenove Road meets the Upper Clapton Road. He was walking up this road when a crazy kid, who'd stolen a car, swerved from the main road too fast. **246**

RAMBO 'So there I was riding this horse galloping fast just hanging on to its neck. And she let me. She let me hang on there. She trusted me. We was comfortable together, like we'd always known one another.' **248**

MARVIN 'And there is nothing new under the sun!' says Ecclesiastes who was wrong, wrong, wrong – the morbid old bugger. As I was wrong. Wrong, wrong, wrong! Everyone should be allowed to reinvent the wheel. **248**

INDEX: male/female/age

From *The Kitchen*

Synopsis:

Set in the basement kitchen of a large restaurant, thirty chefs, waitresses, and kitchen porters, slowly begin the day preparing to serve lunch.

The central story tells of a frustrated love affair between a high-spirited, young, German chef, Peter, and a married English waitress, Monique.

Part one slowly builds to a frenzy of serving.

Part two is a lyrical period in which some of the kitchen porters and chefs linger after serving lunch, and talk about their dreams of a better life.

In part three everyone returns for the slower evening service during which Peter, finally turned down by Monique, goes berserk and smashes the gas leads to the ovens.

The proprietor, bewildered by the violence the nature of which he cannot understand, asks his workers what more is there to life than work, money and food.

THE INTERLUDE

> *PAUL is the pastry chef. He's called upon by PETER to outline his 'dream'.*

PAUL   Listen, Peter, I'll tell you something. I'm going to be honest with you. You don't mind if I'm honest? Right, I'm going to be honest with you. I don't like you. Wait, wait a minute – let me finish. I don't like you. I think you're a pig. You bully, you're jealous, you go mad with your work, you always quarrel. All right! But now it's quiet, the ovens are low, the work has stopped for a little and now I'm getting to know you. I still think you're a pig, only now – not so much of a pig. So that's what I dream. I dream of a friend. You give me a rest, you give me silence, you take away this mad kitchen – so I make friends. So I think – maybe all the people I thought were pigs are not so much pigs... Listen, I'll tell you a story. Next door to me, next door where I live is a bus driver.

29

Comes from Hoxton. He's my age, married, got two
kids. He says good morning to me, I ask him how he
is, I give his children sweets. That's our relationship.
Somehow he seems frightened to say too much, you
know? God forbid I might ask him for something. So
we make no demands on each other.

Then one day the busmen go on strike. He's out
for five weeks. Every morning I say to him 'Keep
going, mate, you'll win!' Every morning I give him
words of encouragement, I say I understand his
cause. I've got to get up earlier to get to work but
I don't mind – we're neighbours – we're workers
together – he's pleased.

Then one Sunday there's a peace march. I don't
believe they do much good but I go, because in
this world a man's got to show he can have his say.
The next morning he comes up to me and he says,
now listen to this, he says 'Did you go on that peace
march yesterday?' So I says, yes, I did go on that
peace march yesterday. So then he turns round to
me and he says, 'You know what? A bomb should
have been dropped on the lot of them! It's a pity',
he says, 'that they had children with them 'cos a
bomb should have been dropped on the lot!' And
you know what was upsetting him? The march was
holding up the traffic, the buses couldn't move so
fast!

Now, I don't want him to say I'm right. I don't want
him to agree with what I did – but what terrifies me
is that he didn't stop to think that this man helped
me in my cause so maybe, only *maybe*, there's
something in *his* cause – I'll talk about it. No! The
buses were held up so drop a bomb, he says, on
the lot! And you should have seen the hate in his
eyes, as if I'd murdered his child. Like an animal he
looked. And the horror is this – that there's a wall,
a big wall between me and millions of people like
him. And I think – where will it end? What do you
do about it? And I look around me, at the kitchen,

at the factories, at the enormous bloody buildings going up with all those offices and all those people in them, and I think – Christ! I think, Christ, Christ, Christ!

I agree with you, Peter – maybe one morning we *should* wake up and find them all gone. But then I think: I should *stop* making pastries? The factory worker should stop making trains and cars? The miner should leave the coal where it is? (*Pause.*) *You* give *me* an answer. You give me *your* dream.

From *Chicken Soup with Barley*

Synopsis:

The play spans twenty years – 1936 to 1956 – in the life of the communist Kahn family: Sarah and Harry, and their children, Ada and Ronnie.

Beginning with the anti-fascist demonstrations in 1936 in London's East End and ending with the Hungarian uprising in 1956, the play explores the theme of political disillusionment parallelled with the disintegration of a family.

It is the son, Ronnie, who is the most deeply affected and turns on his mother for insisting on remaining a communist. Her reply ends the play on a note of desperate optimism.

ACT THREE SCENE ONE

SARAH   Poor Harry. He's had two strokes. He won't get any better. Paralysed down one side. He can't control his bowels, you know… It's *ach a nebish** Harry now. Not easy for him. But he won't do anything to help himself. I don't know, other men get ill but they fight. Harry's never fought. Funny thing. There were three men like this in the flats, all had strokes. And all three of them seemed to look the same. They walked the same, stooped the same, and all needing a shave. They used to sit outside together and talk for hours on end and smoke. Sit and talk and smoke. That was their life. Then one day one of them decided he wanted to live so he gets up and finds himself a job – running a small shoe-mender's – and he's earning money now. A miracle! Just like that. But the other one – he wanted to die. I used to see him standing outside in the rain, the pouring rain, getting all wet so that he could catch a cold and die. Well, it happened: last week he died. Influenza! He just didn't want to live. But Harry was not like either of them. He didn't want to die but he doesn't

*What-a-pity

seem to care about living. So! What can you do to
help a man like that? I make his food and I buy him
cigarettes and he's happy. My only dread is that he
will mess himself. When that happens I go mad – I
just don't know what I'm doing.

ACT THREE SCENE TWO

SARAH in a quarrel with her son, RONNIE.

SARAH   Alright! So I'm still a communist! Shoot me then!
I'm a communist! I've always been one – since
the time when all the world was a communist. You
know that? When you were a baby and there was
unemployment and everybody was thinking, so – all
the world was a Communist. But it's different now.
Now the people have forgotten. I sometimes think
they're not worth fighting for because they forget
so easily. You give them a few shillings in the bank
and they can buy a television so they think it's all
over, there's nothing more to be got, they don't have
to think any more! Is that what you want? A world
where people don't think any more? Is that what
you want me to be satisfied with – a television set?
Look at him! My son! He wants to die!… You want
me to cry again? We should all sit down and cry?…
And he calls me a pathological case! Pop! Pop,
pop, pop, pop – shmop! You think it doesn't hurt
me – the news about Hungary? You think I know
what happened and what didn't happen? Do any of
us know? Who do I know who to trust now – God,
who are our friends now? But all my life I've fought.
With your father and the rotten system that couldn't
help him. All my life I worked with a party that
meant glory and freedom and brotherhood. You
want me to give it up now? You want me to move
to Hendon and forget who I am? If the electrician
who comes to mend my fuse blows it instead, so I
should stop having electricity? I should cut off my
light? Socialism is my light, can you understand

that? A way of life. A man *can* be beautiful. I hate
ugly people – I can't bear meanness and fighting and
jealousy – I've got to have light. I'm a simple person,
Ronnie, and I've got to have light and love. (*Pause.*)
Ah!

You think I didn't love your father enough, don't
you? I'll tell you something. When Ada had
diphtheria and I was pregnant I asked Daddy to
carry her to the hospital. He wouldn't. We didn't
have money because he didn't care to work and
I didn't know what to do. He disappeared. It was
Mrs Bernstein who saved her – you remember
Mrs Bernstein? No, of course not, she died when
you were born. It was Mrs Bernstein's soup. Ada
still has that taste in her mouth – chicken soup
with barley. She says it's a friendly taste – ask her.
That saved her. Not even my brothers had money
in those days, and a bit of dry crust with a cup of
tea – ah! It was wonderful. But Daddy had the relief
money. Someone told me they saw him eating salt
beef sandwiches in Bloom's. He didn't care. Maybe
it was his illness *then* – who knows! He was never
really a bad man. He never beat us or got drunk or
gambled. He wasn't vulgar or coarse and he always
had friends. So what was wrong? *I* could never
understand him. All I did was fight him because
he didn't care. Look at him now. He doesn't care
to live. He's never cared to fully undress himself
and put on pyjamas; never cared to keep shaved
or washed; or be on time or even turn up! And
now he walks around with his fly-buttons and his
shoelaces undone because he still doesn't care to
fight his illness – and the dirt gathers around him.
He doesn't care! And so I fought him because he
didn't care. I fought everybody who didn't care. All
the authorities, the shopkeepers, even today – those
stinking assistance officers – I could buy them with
my little finger – even now I'm still fighting them.
And you want to be like them, like your father?

I'll fight you then... Your father was a weak man.
Could you do any of the things he did?... Ronnie,
your father would never have left his mother to go
abroad as you did. I don't tell you all this now to
pull you down but on the contrary – so you should
know, so you should care. Learn from us, for God's
sake learn from us. What does it matter if your
father was a weakling, or the man you worked with
was an imbecile. They're human beings... There
will always be human beings and as long as there
are there will always be the idea of brotherhood...
Despite the human beings... Despite them!... Alright
then! Nothing, then! It all comes down to nothing!
People come and people go, wars destroy, accidents
kill and plagues starve – it's all nothing, then!
Philosophy? You want philosophy? Nothing means
anything! There! Philosophy! I know! So? Nothing!
Despair – die then! Will that be achievement? To
die? You don't want to do that, Ronnie. So what if
it all means nothing? When you know *that* you can
start again. Please, Ronnie, don't let me finish this
life thinking I lived for nothing. We got through,
didn't we? We got scars but we got through. You
hear me, Ronnie? You've got to care, You've got
to care or you'll die... You'll die, you'll die – if you
don't care you'll die. Ronnie, if you don't care you'll
die.

From *Roots*

Synopsis:

Explores the theme of 'self-discovery'.

Beatie Bryant, daughter of Norfolk farm labourers, has fallen in love with Ronnie Kahn from the 'Chicken Soup' family.

She returns from London to visit her family all of whom await the arrival of Ronnie.

During the two week waiting period Beatie is full of Ronnie's thoughts and words.

At the end of the two weeks the family gather for a huge, specially prepared Saturday afternoon tea to meet him. He doesn't turn up. Instead, with the afternoon post, comes a letter from him saying he doesn't think the relationship will work. The family turn on Beatie.

In the process of defending herself she counter-attacks and instead of using Ronnie's words she finds, to her delight, that she's using her own voice.

ACT THREE

> *The BRYANT front room. The letter from RONNIE has arrived. Everyone feels let down.*

MRS BRYANT I hed enough. All this time she've bin home she've bin tellin' me I didn't do this and I didn't do that and I hevn't understood half what she've said and I've hed enough. She talk about bein' part o' the family but she've never lived at home since she've left school look. Then she go away from here and fill her head wi' high-class squit and then it turn out she don't understand any on it herself. It turn out she do just the same things she say I do. Well, am I right, gal? I'm right ent I? When you tell me I was stubborn, what you mean was that *he* told you *you* was stubborn – eh? When you tell me I don't understand you mean *you* don't understand isn't it? When you tell me I don't make no effort you mean *you* don't make no effort. Well, what you blaming

me for? Blaming me all the time! I haven't bin
responsible for you since you left home – you bin
on your own. She think I like it, she do! Thinks I
like being cooped up in this house all day. Well I'm
telling you my gal – I don't! There! And if I had a
chance to be away working somewhere the whole lot
on you's could go to hell – the lot on you's. Alright
so I am a bloody fool! Alright – so I know it! A
whole two weeks I've bin told it. Well, so then I can't
help you my gal, no that I can't, and you get used to
that once and for all.

ACT THREE

BEATIE   Roots, roots, roots! Christ, Frankie, you're in the
fields all day, you should know about growing
things. Roots! The things you come from, the things
that feed you. The things that make you proud of
yourself – roots!… I'm not talking about family
roots – I mean – the – I mean – Look! Ever since it
begun the world's bin growin' hasn't it? Things hev
happened, things hev bin discovered, people hev bin
thinkin' an' improvin' an' inventin' but what do we
know about it all?… What do you mean 'what am I
on about'? I'm talkin'! Listen to me!

I'm tellin' you that the world's bin growin' for
thousands of years and we haven't noticed it. I'm
tellin' you that we don't know what we are or where
we come from. I'm tellin' you something's cut us
off from the beginning. I'm tellin' you we've got no
roots. Blimey Joe! We've all got large allotments, we
all grow things around us so we should know about
roots. You know how to keep your flowers alive
don't you, mother? Jimmy – you know how to keep
the roots of your veggies strong and healthy. It's not
only the corn that need strong roots, you know, it's
us too. But what've we got? Go on, tell me, what've
we got? We don't know where we push up from and
we don't bother neither…

You say you aren't grumblin' – oh yes, you say so,
but look at you. What've you done since you come
in? Hev you said anythin'? I mean really said or
done anythin' to show you're alive? Alive! Blust,
what do it mean? Do you know what it mean? Any
on you? Shall I tell you what Susie said when I went
and saw her? She say she don't care if that ole atom
bomb drop and she die – that's what she say. And
you know why she say it? I'll tell you why, because
if she had to care she'd have to do something about
it and she find *that* too much effort. Yes she do. She
can't be bothered – she's too bored with it all. That's
what we all are – we're all too bored…

Oh yes, we turn on a radio or a TV set maybe,
or we go to the pictures – if them's love stories
or gangsters – but isn't that the easiest way out?
Anything so long as we don't have to make an effort.
Well, am I right? You know I'm right. Education ent
only books and music – it's askin' questions, all the
time. There are millions of us, all over the country,
and no one, not one of us, is askin' questions, we're
all takin' the easiest way out. Everyone I ever
worked with took the easiest way out. We don't fight
for anythin', we're so mentally lazy we might as well
be dead. Blust, we are dead! And you know what
Ronnie say sometimes? He say it serves us right!
That's what he say – it's our own bloody fault!…

Oh, he thinks we *count* all right – livin' in 'mystic
communion with nature'. Livin' in mystic bloody
communion with nature (indeed). But us count?
Count, mother? I wonder. Do we? Do you think we
really count? You don' wanna take any notice of
what them ole papers say about the workers bein'
all-important these days – that's all squit! 'Cos we
aren't. Do you think when the really talented people
in the country get to work they get to work for us?
Hell if they do? Do you think they don't know we
'ont make the effort? The writers don't write thinkin'
we can understand, nor the painters don't paint

expectin' us to be interested – that they don't, nor
don't the composers give out music thinkin' we can
appreciate it. 'Blust,' they say, 'the masses is too
stupid for us to come down to them. Blust,' they
say, 'if they don't make no effort why should we
bother?' So you know who come along? The slop
singers and the pop writers and the film makers
and the women's magazines and the Sunday papers
and the picture-strip love stories – thaas who come
along, and you don't hev to make no effort for them,
it come easy. 'We know where the money lie,' they
say, 'hell we do! The workers have got it so let's give
them what they want. If they want slop songs and
film idols we'll give 'em that then. If they want words
of one syllable, we'll give 'em that then. If they
want the third-rate, *blust*! We'll give 'em *that* then.
Anything's good enough for them 'cos they don't ask
for no more!' the whole stinkin' commercial world
insults us and we don't care a damn. Well Ronnie's
right – it's our own bloody fault. We want the
third-rate – we got it! We got it! We got it! We…

*Suddenly BEATIE stops as if listening to herself. She
pauses, turns with an ecstatic smile on her face –*

D'you hear that? D'you hear it? Did you listen to
me? I'm talking. Jenny, Frankie, Mother – I'm not
quoting no more… Listen to me someone.

As though a vision were revealed to her.

God in heaven, Ronnie! It does work, it's happening
to me, I can feel it's happened, I'm beginning, on my
own two feet – I'm beginning…

From *I'm Talking About Jerusalem*

Synopsis:

Ada Kahn, the daughter of the 'Chicken Soup' family, marries Dave Simmonds. They move to an isolated house in Norfolk where they struggle through a back-to-the-land experiment. Dave makes furniture by hand.

Friends and family visit them throughout their twelve rural years charting and commenting on the fortunes of their experiment. It doesn't work, but they end deeply gratified to have had the courage to try.

ACT ONE SCENE TWO

> *LIBBY DOBSON is an old Air Force friend of DAVE's on a visit. Tension between him and ADA.*

DOBSON I've tried it, Dave – listen to me and go home – I've tried it and failed. Socialism? I didn't sell out that easily. You've gone back to William Morris, but I went back to old Robert Owen. Five thousand pounds my old man left me, and I blushed when I heard it. But I still hung on. It's not mine, I decided – the profits of exploitation, I said. Right! Give it back! So I worked out a plan. I found four other young men who were bright mechanics like myself and who were wasting their talents earning ten pounds a week in other men's garages, and I said 'Here's a thousand pounds for each of you – no strings, no loans, it's yours! Now let's open our own garage and exploit no one but ourselves. There's only one provision,' I said, 'only one: as soon as there is an excess profit of another thousand pounds, we find someone else to inherit it and we expand that way!' See the plan? A chain of garages owned and run by the workers themselves, the real thing, and I will build it myself. Can you imagine what a bloody fool they must have thought me? Can you guess the hell of a time they had planning to buy me out? Democracy, mate? I spit it! Benevolent dictatorship for me. You want Jerusalem? Order it with an iron hand – no questions, no speeches for and against – bang! It's there! You don't understand it? You don't want it? Tough luck, comrade – your children will! (*To ADA.*) No peace? You're right, Mrs Simmonds. I'm dirtied up. Listen to me, Dave, and go home before you're dirtied up…

What? Is that all you can say, Ada? I've just related a modern tragedy and you're warning me against alcohol. She's a real woman this Ada of yours. A woman dirties you up as well, you know. She and the world – they change you, they bruise you, they dirty you up – between them, you'll see… Oh no, you mean you've had enough. The little woman senses danger – marvellous instinct for self-preservation. I suppose you two consider you are happily married for ever and ever and ever. I was married once. God knows how it happened – just after demob. I used to watch her as the weeks and months went by; I used to sit and watch fascinated and horrified as – she changed. This was before the old man died and we both went out to work. After supper we'd wash up and she'd sit by the fire and fall asleep. Just fall asleep – like that. She might glance at a newspaper or do a bit of knitting, but nothing else – nothing that might remind me she was alive. And her face would go red in front of the fire and she'd droop around and be slovenly. And I just watched her. She chewed food all the time, you know. Don't believe me? I watched her! Chewing all the time. Even in bed, before she went to sleep – an apple or a piece of gateau – as though terrified she wasn't getting enough into her for that day.

And she became so gross, so indelicate, so unfeeling about everything. All the grace she had was going, and instead there was flesh growing all around her. I used to sit and watch it grow. How does one ever know, for Christ's sake, that a woman carries the seeds of such disintegration?

Then I tried what your brother wants to do – take a
simple girl, a girl from an office, lively, uncluttered.
Wife number two! Just about the time I inherited
my five thousand pounds. A real socialist enterprise
and a simple wife. Ironic, really. There was I putting
a vision into practice, and there was she watching
me in case I looked at other women – making me
feel lecherous and guilty. *She's* the kind that dirties
you up. There was I sharing out my wealth and
there was she – always wanting to possess things,
terrified of being on her own. She marries a man
in order to have something to attach to herself, a
possession! The man provides a home – bang! She's
got another possession. *Her* furniture, *her* saucepans,
her kitchen – bang! Bang! Bang! And then she has a
baby – bang again! All possessions!

And this is the way she grows. She grows and she
grows and she grows and she takes from a man
all the things she once loved him for – so that no
one else can have them – because you see, the
more she grows, ah! the more she needs to protect
herself. Clever? Bloody clever! I think I hate women
because they have no vision. Remember that,
Davey – they haven't really got vision, only a sense
of self-preservation. And you will get smaller and
smaller and she will grow and grow and you will
be able to explain nothing because everything else
will be a foreign language to her. You know? Those
innocent I-don't-know-what-you're-talking-about
eyes?

ACT TWO SCENE ONE

ADA has returned from visiting her father, HARRY, in hospital where he's recovering from a stroke that's affected his brain.

ADA He didn't recognise me at first. He was lying on his back. You know how large his eyes are – they couldn't focus on anything. He kept shouting in Yiddish, calling for his mother and his sister, Cissy. Mummy told me he was talking about Russia. It seems when they first brought him into the ward he threw everything about – that's why a padded cell. He looked so frightened and mad, as if he were frightened of his own madness… A clot of blood. It's reached the brain.

And then he recognised me and he looked at me and I said 'hello Daddy, it's Ada' and he started screaming in Yiddish '*Dir hasst mir, dir hasst mir, dir host mirch alle mul gerhasst!*' You hate me and you've always hated me. (*Weeps uncontrollably.*) Oh darling, I haven't stopped crying and I don't understand it, I don't understand it because it's not true, it's never been true… He smiled and kissed me a lot before I left, it was an uncanny feeling, but you know, Dave, I feel like a murderer… No, of course I don't think I was responsible for his illness and neither did I hate him. But perhaps I didn't tell him I loved him. Useless bloody things words are. Ronnie and his bridges! 'Words are bridges' he wrote, 'to get from one place to another.' Wait till he's older and he learns about silences – they span worlds…

Bridges! What bridges? Do you think I know what words go to make *me*? Do you think I know why I behave the way I behave? Everybody says I'm cold and hard, people want you to cry and gush over them. During the war, when you were overseas, I used to spend nights at home with Sarah and the family. There was never a great deal of money

coming in and Mummy sometimes got my shopping
and did my ironing. Sometimes she used to sit up
late with me while I wrote to you in Ceylon, and she
used to chatter away and then – fall asleep. She'd sit
in the chair, straight up, and fall asleep. And every
time she did that and I looked at her face it was so
sweet, so indescribably sweet that I'd cry. There!
Each time she fell asleep I'd cry. But yet I find it
difficult to talk to her. So there! Explain it! Use words
and explain that to me… My mother is a strong
woman, Dave. She was born to survive every battle
that faces her. She doesn't need me. You say I'm
like her? You're right. I'm also strong, I shall survive
every battle that faces me too, and this place means
survival for me. We-are-staying-put!

ACT TWO SCENE TWO

*ESTHER is one of ADA's two maiden aunts who are
visiting them.*

ESTHER   My mother loved her children. You know how I
know? The way she used to cook our food. With
songs. She used to hum and feed us. Sing and dress
us. Coo and scold us. You could tell she loved us
from the way she did things for us. You want to be
a craftsman? Love us. You want to give us beautiful
things? Talk to us. You think Cissie and I fight?
You're wrong silly boy. She talks to me. I used to
be able to watch everything on television but she
moaned so much I can't even enjoy rubbish any
more. She drives me mad with her talk… You think
working with hands is the only way to work? I'm a
worker too. Haven't I worked? From selling flags at a
football match to selling foam cushions in Aylesbury
Market. From six in the morning till six at night.
From pitch to pitch, all hours, all my life! That's not
work? It doesn't entitle me to a house? Or a fridge?
I shouldn't buy a washing machine? How do you
measure achievement for Christ's sake? Flower and

Dean Street was a prison with iron railings, you remember? And my one ambition was to break away from that prison. 'Buy your flags' I used to yell. 'Rattles at rattling good prices' I used to try to be funny. So I sold rattles and now I've got a house. And if I'd've been pretty I'd've had a husband and children as well and they'd've got pleasure from me. Did money change me? You remember me, tell me, have I changed? I'm still the same Esther Kahn. I've got no airs. No airs, me. I still say the wrong things and nobody minds me. Look at me – you don't like me or something? That's all that matters. Or no, not that, not even like or dislike – do I harm you? Do I offend you? Is there something about me that offends you?

ACT TWO SCENE THREE

DAVE and ADA are packing up. As with their arrival SARAH and RONNIE are there to help them. RONNIE is gloomy over what he considers is ignominious retreat.

DAVE   What do you think I am, Ronnie? You think I'm an artist's craftsman? Nothing of the sort. A designer? Not even that. Designers are ten a penny. I don't mind Ronnie – believe me I don't. (*But he does.*) I've reached the point where I can face the fact that I'm not a prophet. Once I had – I don't know – a – a moment of vision, and I yelled at your Aunty Esther that I was a prophet. A prophet! Poor woman, I don't think she understood. All I meant was I was a sort of spokesman. That's all. But it passed. Look, I'm a bright boy. There aren't many flies on me and when I was younger I was even brighter. I was interested and alive to everything, history, anthropology, philosophy, architecture – I had ideas. But not now. Not now Ronnie. I don't know – it's sort of sad this what I'm saying, it's a sad time for both of us – Ada and me – sad, yet – you know – it's not all that bad. We came here, we worked hard, we've loved every minute of it and we're still young. Did you expect anything else? You wanted us to grow to be giants, didn't you? The mighty artist craftsman! Well, now the only things that seem to matter to me are the day-to-day problems of my wife, my kids and my work. Face it – as an essential member of society I don't really count. I'm not saying I'm useless, but machinery and modern techniques have come about to make me the odd man out. Here I've been, comrade citizen, presenting my offerings and the world's rejected them. I don't count, Ronnie, and if I'm not sad about it you mustn't be either. Maybe Sarah's right, maybe you can't build on your own.

From *Chips With Everything*

Synopsis:

Early 1950s. A group of Air Force conscripts are assembled to begin eight weeks of 'square-bashing' – basic military drill.

Two of the conscripts develop a relationship, Pip Thompson – an arrogant aristocrat; Chas – a working class boy who secretly admires him.

The military hierarchy want Pip to become an officer. At first he rebelliously refuses. The officers undermine him by corrupting his motives, they tolerate his rebellion and thus defuse it. His spirit is broken. The other recruits rebel just as Pip accepts to become an officer. He in turn urges the military to tolerate them and, in the same way, defuse their rebelliousness. It's a betrayal of the conscripts he has befriended.

The young recruits who began as a shambles end as an efficient, closely linked and acquiescent squad.

ACT ONE SCENE ONE

CORPORAL

HILL   That's better. In future, whenever an NCO comes into the hut, no matter who he is, the first person to see him will call out 'NCO! NCO!' Like that. And whatever you're doing, even it you're stark bollock naked, you'll all spring to attention as fast as the wind from a duck's arse, and by Christ that's fast. Is that understood? (*No reply.*) Well is it? (*A few murmurs.*) When I ask a question I expect an answer. (*Emphatically.*) Is that understood?

     They all shout a reply 'Yes, Corporal'.

Better! Anyone been in the Air Cadets? Any of the cadets? Anyone twenty-one or more then? Nineteen? Month you were born? Right, you're senior man. And you're assistant. Shift your kit to the top of the hut. Not now – later.

Now, see these small boys, these two, they're my boys. They'll do the jobs I ask them when I ask

them; not much, my fires each day, perhaps my
bunk – my boys. But they won't do my polishing – I
do that myself. No one is to start on them, no one
is to bully them, if they do, then they answer to me.
You can sit.

Right, you're in the RAF now, you're not at home.
This hut, this place here, this is going to be your
home for the next eight fucking weeks. This billet
here, you see it? This? It's in a state now, no one's
been in it for the last four days so it's in a state now.
(*Pause.*) But usually it's like a fucking palace! (*Pause.*)
That's the way I want it to be 'cos that's the way it's
always been. Now you've got to get to know me.
My name is Corporal Hill. I'm not a very happy
man, I don't know why. I never smile and I never
joke – you'll soon see that. Perhaps it's my nature,
perhaps it's the way I've been brought up – I don't
know. The RAF brought me up. You're going to go
through hell while you're here, through fucking hell.
Some of you will take it and some of you will break
down. I'm warning you – some of you shall end up
crying. And when that happens I don't want to see
anyone laughing at him. Leave him alone, don't
touch him.

But I'll play fair. You do me proud and I'll play
fair. The last lot we ad 'ere 'ad a good time, a right
time, a right good fucking time. We 'ad bags o' fun,
bags o' it. But I will tear and mercilessly scratch the
fucking daylights out of anyone who smarts the alec
with me – and we've got some 'ere. I can see them,
you can tell them. I count three already, you can tell
them, by their faces, who know it all, the boys who
think they're GOOD. (*Whispered.*) It'll be unmerciful
and fucking murder for them – all. Now, you see this
wireless here, this thing with knobs and a pretty light
that goes on and off? Well that's ours, our wireless
for this hut, and for this hut only because this hut
has always been the best hut. No other hut has a
wireless. I want to keep that. I like music and I want

to keep that wireless. Some people, when they get
up in the morning, first thing all they want to do is
smoke, or drink tea – not me, I've got to have music,
the noise of instruments.

Everyone's got a fad, that's mine, music, and I want
to be spoilt, you see to it that I'm spoilt. Right, if
there's anyone here who wants to leave my hut and
go into another because he doesn't like this 'un, then
do it now, please. Go on, pick up your kit and move.
I'll let 'im. (*No movement.*) You can go to the Naafi
now. But be back by ten thirty, 'cos that's fucking
lights out. (*Moves to door, pauses.*) Anyone object to
swearing? (*No reply. Exit.*)

ACT ONE SCENE TWO

> *PIP is taunted by the other conscripts with whom he
> shares the hut. Unperturbed, confident with his class,
> he defends himself.*

PIP   Look old son, you're going to have me for eight
painful weeks in the same hut, so spend the next five
minutes taking the mickey out of my accent, get it
off your chest and then put your working-class halo
away because no one's going to care – OK?

You want it straight? I was born in a large country
house, my father is a banker, we idolise each other,
and I'm fucking rich.

One day, when I was driving to my father's office,
the car broke down. I could have got a taxi I
suppose, but I didn't. I walked. The office was in
the City, so I had to walk through the East End,
strange – I don't know why I should have been
surprised. I'd seen photographs of this Mecca
before – I even used to glance at the *Daily Mirror*
now and then, so God knows why I should have
been surprised. Strange. I went into a café and
drank a cup of tea from a thick, white, cracked
cup, and ate a piece of tasteless currant cake. On

the walls I remember they had photographs of
boxers, autographed, and they were curling at
the edges from the heat. Every so often a woman
used to come to the table and wipe it with a rag
that left dark streaks behind which dried up into
weird patterns. Then a man came and sat next to
me – WHY should I have been surprised? I'd seen
his face before, a hundred times on the front pages
of papers reporting a strike. A market man, a porter
or a docker. No, he was too old to be a docker. His
eyes kept watering, and each time they did that he'd
take out a neatly folded handkerchief, unfold it and,
with one corner, he'd wipe away the moisture, and
then he'd neatly fold it up again and replace it in
his pocket. Four times he did that, and each time he
did it he looked at me and smiled. I could see grains
of dirt in the lines of his face, and he wore an old
waistcoat with pearl buttons. He wasn't untidy, the
cloth even seemed a good cloth, and though his hair
was thick with oil it was clean. I can even remember
the colour of the walls, a pastel pink on the top half
and turquoise blue on the bottom, peeling. Peeling
in fifteen different places, actually, I counted them.
But what I couldn't understand was why I should
have been so surprised. It wasn't as though I had
been cradled in my childhood. And then I saw the
menu, stained with tea and beautifully written by a
foreign hand, and on top it said – God I hated that
old man – it said 'Chips with everything'. Chips with
every damn thing. You breed babies and you eat
chips with everything.

ACT TWO SCENE SEVEN

> *There is a moment when PIP refuses to use the bayonet in bayonet drill. Its brutality offends him. And he wants to rebel against his class. His officers recognise he belongs to them and that his refusal is merely youthful rebellion.*

PILOT OFFICER It goes right through us, Thompson. Nothing you can do will change that. We listen but we do not hear, we befriend but do not touch you, we applaud but do not act – to tolerate is to ignore. What did you expect, praise from the boys? Devotion from your mates? Your mates are morons, Thompson, morons. At the slightest hint from us they will disown you. Or perhaps you wanted a court martial? Too expensive, boy. Jankers? That's for the yobs. You, we shall make an officer, as we promised. I have studied politics as well, you know, and let me just remind you of a tactic the best of revolutionaries have employed. That is to penetrate the enemy and spread rebellion there. You can't fight us from the outside. Relent boy, at least we understand long sentences…

Not cynicism – just honesty. I might say we are being unusually honest – most of the time it is unnecessary to admit all this, and you of all people should have known it…

Ah. A touch of anger, what do you reveal now, Thompson? We know, you and I, don't we? Comradeship? Not that, not because of the affinity of one human being to another, not that. Guilt? Shame because of your fellow beings' suffering? You don't feel that either. Not guilt. An inferiority complex, a feeling of modesty? My God. Not that either. There's nothing humble about you, is there? Thompson, you wanted to do more than simply share the joy of imparting knowledge to your friends; no, not modesty. Not that. What then? What if not those things, my lad? Shall I say it? Shall I? Power. Power,

isn't it? Among your own people there were too
many who were powerful, the competition was too
great, but here, among lesser men – here among the
yobs, among the good-natured yobs, you could be
king. KING. Supreme and all powerful, eh? Well?
Not true? Deny it – deny it, then. We know – you
and I – we know, Thompson...

God? God? Why do you call upon God? Are you his
son? Better still, then. You are found out even more,
illusions of grandeur, Thompson. We know that also,
that's what we know, that's what we have, the picture
you have of yourself, and now that we know that,
you're really finished, destroyed. You're destroyed,
Thompson. No man survives whose motive is
discovered, no man.

Messiah to the masses! Huh!

Corporal Hill!

ACT TWO SCENE TEN

*SMILER is one of nature's clumsy creatures. He can
get nothing right in the drilling.*

*As the pass-out parade draws nearer the discipline
becomes more strict. He's bullied by the NCOs and
decides to run away.*

*He's on the run now, running in one spot, simulating
flight.*

SMILER LEAVE ME ALONE! Damn your mouths and
hell on your stripes – leave me alone. Mad they
are, they're mad they are, they're raving lunatics
they are. CUT IT! STUFF IT! Shoot your load on
someone else, take it out on someone else, why do
you want to pick on me, you lunatics, you bloody
apes, you're nothing more than bloody apes,
so damn your mouths and hell on your stripes!
Ahhhhh – they'd kill me if they had the chance.
They think they own you, think that anyone who's

dressed in blue is theirs to muck about, degrade.
YOU BLOODY APES, YOU WON'T DEGRADE
ME! Oh my legs – I'm going home. I'll get a lift and
scarper home. I'll go to France, I'll get away. I'LL
GET AWAY FROM YOU, YOU APES! They think
they own you – Oh my back.

I don't give tuppence what you say, you don't
mean anything to me, your bloody orders nor
your stripes not your jankers nor your wars. Stick
your jankers on the wall, stuff yourselves, go
away and stuff yourselves, stuff your rotten stupid
selves – Ohh – Ohhh.

Look at the sky, look at the moon, Jesus look at that
moon and the frost in the air. I'll wait. I'll get a lift in
a second or two, it's quiet now, their noise is gone.
I'll stand and wait and look at that moon.

What are you made of, tell me? I don't know what
you're made of, you go on and on. What grouses
you? What makes you scream? You're blood and
wind like all of us, what grouses you? You poor duff
bastards, where are your mothers? Where were you
born – I don't know what grouses you, your voices
sound like dying hens – I don't know.

That bloody lovely moon is cold, I can't stay here.
I'll freeze to death. That's a laugh, now that'd fool
them. Listen! A bike, a motor-bike, a roaring bloody
motor-bike. (*Starts thumbing.*) London, London,
London, London, LONDON! (*The roar comes and
dies.*) You stupid ghet, I want a lift, can't you see I
want a lift, an airman wants a lift back home. Home,
you bastard, take me ho'ooooome.

Now they'll catch me, now they'll come, not much
point in going on, Smiler boy, they'll surely come,
they're bound to miss you back at camp – eyes like
hawks they've got – God! Who cares. 'Stop your silly
smiling, Airman' – 'It's not a smile, Corp, it's natural,
honest, Corp. I'm born that way. Honest Corp, it's
not a smile…'

From *The Four Seasons*

Synopsis:

Adam and Beatrice have been bruised by their separate marriages and love affairs and have now agreed to spend time together in a remote cottage, a kind of sabbatical from life.

In Winter she is catatonic. He must attend to things. By the Spring his caring and attention have thawed her frozen feelings. When Summer comes they are in love, and Beatrice begs Adam to come away and begin a new life together in the real world. He hesitates, afraid. They linger till Autumn.

Mistakes which destroyed previous relationships are repeated. Love dies.

SPRING

> *ADAM, full of gaiety, is trying to teach BEATRICE to sing. She claims to be tone deaf. He can't accept this, and presses till she is distressed.*

BEATRICE I can't, I can't, that's it. I can't. No sound, I make no sounds, just a long moan, or a silence. I destroyed a marriage and failed a lover, now leave me alone, damn you. Leave me alone… I just can't sing… I never could… You think I haven't tried? I've tried and tried, I just can't… Nothing!

There was nothing he or I could touch either that didn't explode. What battles we fought. I thought I saw 'God' in him but we fought. The boy with wings! I used to sit at his feet, literally, curled on the floor, hugging him. 'Get up' he'd say, he hated it. 'Get up, off your knees, no woman should be on her knees to a man'. He never believed he was worth such devotion. It embarrassed him.

And I was dead, a piece of nothing until he touched me, or spoke to me, or looked at me. Even his look was an embrace. I used to nag him for all his thoughts, hungry for everything that passed through his mind, jealous that he might be thinking something he couldn't share with me. I couldn't take my eyes off him. I knew every curve, every movement his features made. I don't know why we fought.

That's a lie. I knew very well why we fought. Exclusivity! I couldn't bear to see the shadow of another person fall on him. Even hearing him talk to someone else on the phone about 'ways to mend the world' was enough to make prickles of the hair on my neck. How dare he think *my* intellect was not enough to set to right his silly world's intolerable pain! Do you know what I used to do? Sneer! I used to sneer and denigrate anyone who was near and dear to him – friends, relatives, colleagues. Even his children, I couldn't bear the demands they made on him. When they were desperately ill I dismissed their complaints as childish maladies, and when they cried because their father constantly stayed away I accused them of artfulness. No one missed the whip of my sneers.

But – he was a leader of men, and leaders of men fight back. Every word became a sword, a bomb destroying nerve centres, crippling the heart. We hurled anything at each other: truths, lies, half-truths, what did it matter as long as it was poison, as long as we gave each other no peace. Sometimes he would give in, for love of me, and when the next battle came round I would taunt him with his previous surrender. And when he didn't surrender I would accuse him of being afraid of his wife. No peace, none at all, neither for him nor myself.

Human communication difficult? Not for us it wasn't. We communicated only too well. In the end – we were demented. And for what? A love so desperate that we fought for it not to be recognised, terrified that we might reveal to each other how helpless we were. Isn't that madness? That's madness for you, since without love I've neither appetite nor desire. I'm capable of nothing. And I haven't the strength to forgive myself.

There, can you still teach me to sing? Teach me to love myself better – then perhaps I'll sing.

SUMMER

After BEATRICE, in a burst of exhilarated joy, has asked him to come away with her to start a new life together, he declares he's not yet ready, and explains why.

ADAM   Two kinds of love, two kinds of women. The woman whose love embraces you, the woman whose love oppresses you. The first keeps its distance, and you emerge slowly, confidently. The second burns the air around you till you can't breathe or speak.

You know, when I was born I was born with a great laughter in me. Can you believe that? A great laughter, like a blessing. And some people loved and some people hated it. It was a sort of challenge, a test against which people measured themselves; and I could never understand the extremes of either their love or their hate.

Have you ever been with a beautiful woman, a really breathtaking beauty, and watched the passionate waves of devotion and loathing she attracts? Noticed how the people around feel the irresistible need to say sly, unpleasant things to show they're not intimidated by her beauty? So it was with my laughter.

And she, who had no need to measure herself against anything or anyone because she was endowed with her own loveliness, her own intelligence – she too began measuring herself against that laughter. And why? Because I was *born* with it, *she* hadn't bestowed it. She couldn't bear that.

She found enemies where there were none, saw betrayals in every act, broke each smile, stormed every moment of peace we'd built. And once, when I cursed her from a sick bed, when *I* lost control, then *she* became calm and took control. Only she could nurse me back to health, you see. 'You' she said, 'are incapable'.

Soon, she made no sense. 'I see God in you' she'd say one day, and the next pour sourness on my work. She'd rave and regret, applaud and destroy, love and devour. Mad! Mad, mad, mad woman! *Why* does a woman destroy her love with such desperate possessiveness, why? She had no need to be desperate – I *was* possessed!

And yet, despite what she is, there's a part of her doesn't deserve what she is. Through all that madness – and it *is* a madness you know, love like that, a madness – but through it all I understood her need to howl. Pain. Such a tortuous relationship. And she understood, also. In moments of peace we both understood and comforted each other. But then she'd forget and howl again, such terror in her voice, such venomous poison. And it went on and on and on and on, relentlessly, crippling us both.

Where is she now, I wonder? Lonely, for sure. Lost somewhere and lonely. No one has the right to take away laughter from a man, or deny a woman her beauty. Lonely, unutterably lonely.

And me? 'Me' rummages about the world looking for bits and pieces of old passions, past enthusiasms, echoes of old laughter. A feeble search, really. I see things wanting her to see them. I visit places wanting her to be with me. I think thoughts wanting her to share them, crying out for her praise. All that I do, everything, is a pale reflection of her taste, her vivid personality.

We never recover, do we? With her the laughter
became cries of pain; without her the laughter is
gone. We never really recover.

SUMMER

*BEATRICE has a fierce tongue. They quarrel. When one
is ready to love the other is not. After one such quarrel
ADAM becomes ill. BEATRICE nurses him.*

BEATRICE   I'm here, my lovely one, right here. No need to cry
out. Hush. Lie still, I'm here, feel me.

*He settles. She places a blanket round her shoulders
awaiting his recovery.*

How I wish I could sing now.

You're right, it *is* a kind of crippling when your
voice can't make music. You know, I'm not really
as treacherous as I sound, or cold or humourless.
Sometimes a fever gets in me too and I don't know
what I say. But I'm always honest, at least to myself,
and good and really – very wise.

But I'm damaged. I blush for the creases in my
skin. Worn limbs, second-hand. Third-hand to
be precise; third-hand, bruised and damaged – I
wheeze and whirr, like a clock striking the wrong
hour – midnight when it's only six.

But if we'd met before meeting anyone else,
then – Oh, Adam, the right hour would have struck
at the right time, every time, clear and ringing. If, if,
if…and what wouldn't we have done together then,
eh? Raised storms among the dead, that's what we'd
have done, then.

Do you know what my husband said to me? 'You're
like a queen,' he said, 'without her country. I hate
queens,' he said, 'without their countries.' And he
was right. No home and no man to pay me homage.
All my life I've looked for peace and majesty, for a
man who was unafraid and generous; generous and

not petty. I can't bear little men; mean, apologetic, timid men; men who mock themselves and sneer at others; who delight in downfall and dare nothing. Peace, majesty and great courage – how I've longed for these things.

He once abandoned me in a fog, that man, that man I called 'God'; in a long, London fog, left me, to walk home alone.

Peace, majesty and great courage.

And once I ran through a storm and stood on a station platform, soaking and full of tears, pleading with him to take me, take me, take me with him. And he wanted to take me, I know it, because we loved walking through streets in strange towns, discovering new shapes to the houses, breathing new airs. But he refused to show his need.

Peace, majesty and great courage – never. I've found none of these things. Such bitter disappointment. Bitter! Bitter, bitter, bitter! And out of such bitterness cruelty grows. You can't understand the cruelty that grows. And I meant none of it, not one cruel word of it. And he knew and I knew and we both knew that we knew, but the cruelty went on.

Still, 'laments' for what's done and past won't cure the invalid will they? I should be making plans for tomorrow shouldn't I? For when you get up, and the day after, and the month after, and all those long years we'll have together. What shall we do in those years, Adam? Eh? All those great, long years ahead? I have plans, you know, children, travel, daring all those things you didn't dare before. We'll plot each moment. Two brilliant lovers.

And peace, above all – peace, and trust and majesty and all that great courage.

Get well, darling boy. My voice may not sing but my love does. Get well.

From *Their Very Own And Golden City*

Synopsis:

Andrew Cobham, an apprentice draughtsman, and his young friends from Durham spend a day sketching in Durham Cathedral. On entering, Andrew is overwhelmed. As though by osmosis he knows that one day he will become an architect. The year is 1926.

He and his friends talk about the future that is all before them, to do with as they please – so they imagine. They will build six beautiful cities, which will be paid for and owned by the people who live in them, and industry will be capitalised by the Trade Unions.

As they plan it, the future unfolds.

In the beginning all happens as they plan. We keep returning to them in the Cathedral, always full of hope and more plans. Until, at a certain moment, we see their future swerve in a different direction. Reality, in conflict with The Dream, moves away from it.

Only one city is built, beautiful but not as they had envisioned it. Andrew is knighted and moves towards the end of his life feeling he has compromised, failed. The year is now 1985.

But the play ends in 1926, in the Cathedral, with youth's hopes. The Dream remains. We have only 'flashed forward'.

ACT ONE SCENE FIVE

>*ANDREW meets JAKE LATHAM, an eminent trade union leader, who becomes his mentor but who he later has to betray.*

JAKE   I don't know what to teach you, lad, daft old man, me. I'm a bit overwhelmed perhaps. It must have been the vanity of old age made me invite you here. I'm not a teacher. I've got a pocket full of principles, that's all, really. If you'd tried to answer my question I'd have tried to apply those principles, but… There *was* a principle involved in that crisis you know. It wasn't very widely argued but it was there.

Do you know what the Bank of England did – poor
bloody Ramsay MacDonald – they frightened the
pants off him. All our gold was going, you see,
flowing out of the window it was, people drawing
left, right and centre. So the directors of the Bank
demanded to see the Prime Minster and give him
their view of the situation. And what was their
view? They said to him: 'MacDonald, old son, this
isn't a financial problem, it's a political one. No one
abroad will lend us any money because they are
worried about your government,' they said. 'The
Labour Government,' they said, 'is squandering too
much money on silly things, frivolous things, like
social services and education,' they said. 'Foreigners
don't trust your government, Mr MacDonald, they
don't think you can handle the affairs of the British
nation.' Huh! You wouldn't think that a Labour
Prime Minister would fall for anything as simple as
that, would you?

But he did, old MacDonald. 'You're right,' he
said to the Bank of England. 'We *have* been silly,
I'll make cuts.' So he tried, but he didn't have all
the Cabinet with him, and he resigned, formed
a coalition government and then made the cuts.
It's almost unbelievable, isn't it? Where does the
principle come in? I'll tell you. (*Beginning to get
excited.*) Would it have been unreasonable to expect
a socialist government to apply socialist economic
principles instead of the usual patchwork? It
wouldn't, would it? But did they? (*Mocking.*) 'The
time isn't ripe! The government'll be defeated!'
The sort of answer we all give when we don't do
the things we feel are right. So here's the question:
is it better to risk defeat in defence of a principle
or hang on with compromises?... I tell you,
people always need to know that someone was
around who acted. Defeat doesn't matter; in the
long run all defeat is temporary. It doesn't matter
about present generations but future ones always

want to look back and know that someone was
around acting on principle. That government, I
tell you, should've screamed out to the opposition
'REVOLUTION' – like that. 'Control imports!
Clamp down on speculators! Revolution!' Like
that, at the top of its voice; and then, taken hold of
British industry by the scruff of its neck and made it
develop, themselves, full employment! And perhaps
they'd have crashed – it was a doomed government
anyway – and perhaps we'd have shuddered.
But after the crash, after the shuddering and the
self-pitying and the recriminations, we'd have been
stunned with admiration and the sounds of the
crash would've echoed like bloody great hallelujahs,
bloody great hallelujahs – What the hell you
standing on your head for? You silly or something?
Apoplectic?

ACT TWO SCENE TWO

*KATE is an aristocratic friend of JAKE's. She and
ANDREW draw close as she becomes his ally in the
building of the cities.*

*He feels the people should be asked what kind of
a city they want. She feels that to be a demagogic
approach.*

KATE The common man! What a fraudulent myth – the
glorious age of the common man! My God, this is an
age of flabbiness, isn't it? You know, Stoney, it's not
really the age of the common man, it's the age of the
man who is common, and if it's unforgivable that my
class has produced the myth, then you should weep,
yes weep, that your class has accepted it.

Haven't you noticed how we pat you on the head
at the mere sign of intelligence? 'He reads,' we say;
'how quaint, give him newspapers with large print',
but we keep the leather-bound volumes of poets on
our shelves. Haven't you noticed the patronizing

way we say, 'He's artistic, how touching – give him
pottery classes and amateur theatricals' – but the
masters continue to hang on our walls and the big
theatres are our habitat, not yours. Your homes
are made of brick with crisp square lines and fully
equipped kitchens – but ours are the Georgian
mansions out in the fields and we have rooms for
our guests while you, you have just enough for your
family. You're well fed and there's ample roast beef
at home – but we know the taste of caviar, don't
we? And there are vintage wines on our tables.
And in this day of the man who is common and
drives his Austin and Ford you think you're equal
to any man – but we have the Bentley and the Rolls
and keep quiet because we need to perpetuate the
myth that class differences are past; so we pat his
head and consult the man who is common in the
name of the common man. Questionnaires, Andy?
(*Holding one up.*) Is this what you imagine makes
it the age of the common man? This? (*Reading.*)
'For the people who plan to inhabit the new cities
so that we may know better how to build them.'
Fancy! Architects asking laymen how to build a city.
Why should the man who buys his city know how
to build it? Why shouldn't we turn to you for our
homes, to the poet for his words, to the Church for
its guidance? Participation? It's a sop, dear, to ease
your conscience. Tear them up – be brave, you know
well enough how you want those cities built – shall
we tear them up?

ACT TWO SCENE FIVE, PARTS TWELVE AND THIRTEEN

ANDREW has been knighted. He makes a speech at a reception given in his honour.

ANDY My lords, ladies and gentlemen. I am too old now to begin explaining and excusing the indulgences I allow myself. If the country where I was born and to whom I have given my best, sees fit to honour me, then I must allow it to honour me in the only way it knows how. Having spent a lifetime bullying traditionalists in order to bring into being a revolutionary project, it seems right to stop bullying for a moment and share at least one of the traditions of my opponents.

I suppose I will soon accustom myself to answering to the name, Sir Andrew – we accustom ourselves to anything in old age. No, I mustn't be flippant, I'm honoured, and I'd be churlish and ungracious not to be – yes, churlish and ungracious not to be. After all, the Golden City is built; there were compromises but it's built, a hint, if nothing else, of what could be. It would be churlish and ungracious, (*He coughs.*) very churlish and foolishly ungracious –

ANDY coughs violently.

In walking from the banqueting table to the armchair, ANDY stoops and becomes older. It is many years later. It is ANDY's study.

PART THIRTEEN

He sits a long time alone. Finally –

ANDY I must stop clenching my teeth, I really must try and prevent my teeth from clenching. Howl, that's what I'd do if I opened my mouth – howl. Unclench your teeth, you old fool you. But why is it that I don't want to talk? Because I don't, you know, not a word. One day – I know it – one day I shan't even see people and then what'll happen. I shall stay just still like, petrified, because I won't be able to find a single reason why I should make one word follow another, one thought follow another.

There, look, my teeth are clenched again.

Do you know what depresses me? Men need leaders, that's what depresses me. They'll wait another twenty years and then another leader will come along and they'll build another city. That's all. Patchwork! Bits and pieces of patchwork. Six cities, twelve cities, what difference. Oases in the desert that the sun dries up. Jake Latham, Jake Latham – ah, Jake Latham.

My lifelong boys! *My* lifelong boys? Prefects! That's all; the Labour movement provides prefects to guard other men's principles for living. Oh we negotiate for their better application, shorter working week and all that but – prefects! They need them, we supply them.

Still, nothing wrong in that I suppose; a bargain! A gentlemen's agreement, understood by everybody. They let us build the odd Golden City or two, even help us and in the end – look at me!

I don't suppose there's such a thing as democracy, really, only a democratic way of manipulating power. And equality! None of that either, only a gracious way of accepting inequality.

From *The Friends*

Synopsis:

A group of friends from working-class backgrounds have become very successful designers, and opened many shops selling their designs for interiors. But they find their success hollow because their designs were not bought by the working-class people whom they hoped would respond to 'things of beauty'.

Now they are gathered round one of their number, Esther, who is dying of leukaemia. Death makes them reassess who they are and what they imagined they had achieved. It also, of course, forces them to confront their own mortality.

All the scenes are set in the lounge converted to a bedroom for the dying Esther.

ACT ONE SCENE ONE

> *MANFRED is the brother of ESTHER who is dying.*

MANFRED   You want me to acknowledge the existence of evil, Crispin? Consider this: our trouble, us lot, the once-upon-a-time bright lads from up north, our trouble is that we've no scholarship. Bits and pieces of information, a charming earthiness, intelligence and cheek, but – no scholarship. Look at these books here. (*He picks up a pile and throws them around him.*) Renan, Taine, Kirkegaard, Wittgenstein, Spengler, Plato, Jung, Homer, Vico, Adorno, Lukacs, Heine, Bloch – you've not heard of half of them, have you? And half of them, two-thirds, I'll never read.

Do you know, new knowledge disrupts me. Because there's no solid rock of learning in this thin, undernourished brain of mine, so each fresh discovery of a fact or an idea doesn't replace, it undermines the last; it's got no measurement by which to judge itself, no perspective by which to evaluate its truth or its worth; it can take no proper place in that long view of history scalloped out by

bloody scholarship, because each new concern
renders the last one unimportant. No bloody
scholarship, us. And when I sometimes get a feeling
that two people in love or one man afraid of death
might be a supreme consideration, along comes this
man with his 'we are moving into phases of creative
disorder' and his 'everywhere the lines are blurred'
and I've no defence. He sounds so right, I think, and
besides – he's got scholarship. What's 'silly loving'
and 'banal dying' in all that? Evil? You want me to
confess to the existence of evil? I confess it. I say
it – evil! So? And what shall I do with *that* bit of
knowledge?

ACT ONE SCENE ONE

> *SIMONE is an aristocratic friend who has joined them.*
> *She possesses no skills but was drawn to them by their*
> *talent and energy. She helps run the shops.*
>
> *She's in love with CRISPIN who is cruelly not in love*
> *with her. MACEY is their manager.*

SIMONE The streets are filled with strange, young people,
Macey. Beautiful boys and girls with long hair and
colourful bits and pieces they buy from our shop. All
styles – Victorian, art-nouveau, military – as though
they're attracted by the pomp and circumstance of
traditions they hated – like cats playing with mice
before devouring them. And they want only one
thing, these people. To love. It's as though they're
surrounded by so much ugliness and greed that they
have to spend all their time convincing themselves
that other things exist. And they try to be frightened
of nothing. Anyhow, whatever it is – I'm not much
good at that kind of analysis – two of them came
into the shop today and held out their hands. In one
hand was a black handkerchief containing money,
in the other hand a packet of plain biscuits. And one
of them said, 'Have some money,' like that, 'Have
some money,' as though he were offering me a

cigarette. And do you know I was embarrassed. But
I put my hand into the black handkerchief and took
out two pennies, they were all pennies. 'Now have a
biscuit,' the other one said. I was mesmerized but I
took it, and ate it, and they watched me very closely,
smiling and eager, as though waiting to see if I'd
learned the lesson. Then they walked out, offering
pennies and biscuits to other people. I heard one
person say, 'Not today, thank you.'

ACT ONE SCENE ONE

ESTHER What is it? Why is everyone standing around? I
know what it is. It's depression time again. I'm
dying and you want me to make it easier for you by
pretending I'm not, isn't it? Come on now, we're all
too clever for dramatic deceits like that. And what's
more, your silence and pretending make my misery
worse. Much, much worse. MACEY! I want to go on
living! ROLAND! I *don't* want to die. MANFRED,
SIMONE, TESSA! All of you. I-do-not-want-to-die.
(*Pause.*) My God, that was cruel of me, wasn't it. Oh,
forgive me, everyone, don't take notice. I didn't
mean to give you pain… Yes, I did, I did want to
give pain. I should say I don't mind, make it easier
for you, but I do – I do – I just do. (*Long pause.*)
Manfred I want to walk. Help me. My stick.

Do you know anybody who was prepared to die?
Despite all the suffering and the knowledge of
suffering and man's inhumanity, everyone wants to
go on living – for ever and ever, gloriously.

She slowly circles the room, touching, remembering.

Some people of course know that when they're old
they'll become tired and ready to go; or else they
grow to despise themselves so much for not being
what they thought they were that they become
anxious and eager to fade out. Not me, though.
Just not me. I can't tell you how much I cherish

everything. I know there's a lot that's obscene and ugly but it's never been too oppressive, I've always had the capacity not to be oppressed. *You* know that, don't you, Roland? In the end there's such sweetness, such joy in hidden places. I want to stay on and not miss anything. I want to stay with you, all of you, close and warm and happy. Why shouldn't I want that? And think – all those things I haven't done. Every year the world finds something new to offer me: another man makes music or carves an impossible shape out of the rocks or sings us a poem. Someone is always rising up, taking wing, and behind him he pulls the rest of us; and I want to be there, for every movement, every sound. Why should I want to die away from all that?

That's made me tired again, that has. I keep wanting to talk and I keep getting tired. Manfred, take the pillows away.

ACT ONE SCENE TWO

MANFRED Esther's dying, Macey. We're growing old bit by bit. Every word is a second, passing. It'll never return, never. That's so absolute. I shall never be young again. I shall never laugh the same way again. I shall never love for the first time again, never discover my first sight of the sea, nor climb my first mountain, nor stumble across literature, never; I'll reach out to recapture or remember – but the first ecstasy of all things? Never again. So, it's important. I *must* know. What do I really love? What do I dare to say I despise?

As though trying to remember something he once told himself secretly.

Englishmen! I despise the Englishman. His beliefs embarrass him. (*Pause.*) Is that all I wanted to say? A bit weak, wasn't it? (*Trying again.*) Belief demands passion and passion exposes him so he believes in nothing. He's not terrified of action. Action, battles, defeats – they're easy for him. No, it's ridicule. Passion invites ridicule; men wither from that. Listen to an Englishman talk, there's no real sweetness there, is there? No simplicity, only sneers. The love sneer, the political sneer, the religious sneer – sad. (*Beat.*) Macey's right. We must sell the shop, not fold it up. Sell it and start again, something else. I want to talk about it. Simone, call Tessa and Crispin, drag Roland out from wherever he's crawled – we'll talk, plot. It's so long since we've plotted. (*Long pause.*) Terrible, isn't it? I can't bring myself to believe any of that. Lying there it sounded so logical and right; but saying it, actually using the words – nothing. Stale.

ACT ONE SCENE THREE

MANFRED, with mock seriousness, reads from his notes as though recounting a thriller.

MANFRED *You* thought there were only social revolutions, the French, the industrial and the Russian, eh? Well you're wrong. I've got others for you just as epoch-making. Listen to this. This book tells that in 1600 a man called Gilbert, who was the personal physician to Queen Elizabeth the First, wrote a 'famous' book called *De Magnete* about an electroscope which turned out to be 'indispensable to the development of physical science' and which enabled a man called Thompson to discover that electricity was made of particles which he called electrons, and his discovery had 'the most profound effect on physical science'. 1897! Revolution number one!

And then an American physicist called Millikan measured the electric charge of an electron which led to the extraordinary conclusion that its mass was 1/1835th of a hydrogen atom and thus demonstrated

that particles even *smaller* than atoms existed.
Revolution number two.

Next, a few years later, the Curies! Radium! The
nature of radio-activity revealed! And what was its
nature? Within it, atoms spontaneously exploded!
Out went radiation while behind was left – a
new atom! – thus showing that the immutability
of the elemental atoms was a myth and so
'twentieth-century science was launched on its fateful
journey into the restless world of the atom'. That was
the third revolution.

Now – it gets even more exciting – a man called
Max Planck developed a theory called the
quantum theory which said that radiant heat was
a discontinuous mass made up of particles and *not*
smooth waves, and that was 'so revolutionary' that
even its originator didn't believe it! Einstein had to
prove him right, drawing conclusions which were
themselves revolutionary because he applied Planck's
ideas with 'devastating results to the photo-electric
effect and discovered that light itself also consisted
of multitudes of individual parcels of energy and not
waves'. 'Physicists were incredulous'! It says so here.
(*Taps book.*) 'Incredulous'. Number four and five.

But that was nothing, because he then went on not
to the sixth revolution but to a revolutionary concept
of the very nature of revolutions. He shook the
unshakeable concepts of physics with his famous
theory of relativity which, as we all know, has the
central principle that all natural phenomena are
subject to the same laws for an observer moving
at one speed as they are for another observer
moving at another speed. If you went on a trip
in space you'd return to find your twin brother
older than yourself. 'Common sense mocked' said
the headlines. But man cannot live by theories
alone. While the theorists were theorizing, the
experimentalists were experimenting. Back to the
atom.

Beginning in Manchester and ending in Cambridge
a man called Rutherford, following in the footsteps
of Thompson who, you will remember discovered
the electron, pursued experiments into the nature
of the atom which, he found, was essentially empty!
All that was there was a nucleus of minuscule size
and gargantuan density in which all the atom's mass
was concentrated with electrons orbiting like planets
round the sun. Another revolution is taking shape.

Inspired by Rutherford, a Dane called Niels
Bohr applied quantum theory to the behaviour
of electrons inside atoms in order to understand
how light was born. 'And God said "Let there
be light," and all the little atoms spat out light.'
The revolution shapes on. Not without difficulty
however. Bohr was unable to find the spectra for
complicated atoms and he couldn't account for the
behaviour of extra nuclear electrons in any but the
simplest of atoms. Now, his failure became another
man's challenge, a young German physicist in 1924
called Werner Heisenberg, at the tender age of
twenty-three set out to invent a mathematical theory
which would account for the spectral lines which
could be observed. But – also in 1924 – unknown
to Heisenberg who was courageously going
forward – Louis de Broglie of Paris was going all
the way back. 'Light is waves,' had said everyone.
'No, light is particles' had said Einstein. 'Electrons
are grains of matter,' had said Thompson. 'No,'
de Broglie now said, 'they're trains of waves'. No
revolution is without its problems! The thrilling
microscopic world of the atom refused to behave in
the same way as the mediocre macroscopic world of
man. It was not the same as planets round the sun,
and along came an Austrian physicist called Erwin
Schrödinger to demonstrate it.

Based on de Broglie's conjecture he evolved an
entirely new mathematical approach specifically
designed to describe the behaviour of this incredible

miniature world. Revolutions within revolutions!
But – young Heisenberg was not satisfied with
merely a mathematical description of the dual nature
of the electron and so, in 1927, like Einstein – but
in a different context – he revised the fundamental
meaning of physical measurement. No less! How
does one know anything about atomic particles?
To what extent can we measure them? Can you
measure their properties? The analysis of the
microscopic nature of the atomic world was such
that it drove him to introduce an extraordinary
principle which is called 'the principle of
uncertainty' – very wise! – which states this: 'that
in the nature of things it is impossible to specify
the exact position and the exact velocity of an
electron at the same minute; the uncertainty in the
position could be decreased only by increasing the
uncertainty in the speed or vice-versa;' and guess
what – the product of the two uncertainties turned
out to be a simple multiple of Planck's constant! 'Of
course,' says the book, 'Heisenberg's uncertainty
doesn't affect the behaviour of the world in the gross
but its transformation of the fine detail from an exact
and predictable pattern into a blur of probabilities
was yet another major revolution in scientific
thought!'…

… The revolution approaches its climax. 1930, a
Cambridge mathematician called P A M Dirac. He
synthesizes the physical ideas of Planck, Heisenberg,
de Broglie and Schrödinger, fits them into the
framework of Einstein's theory of relativity and
low and behold – a book called *Relativistic Quantum
Mechanics* in which un dreamt-of phenomena were
revealed such as the creation and annihilation of
particles and antiparticles. It was, this author says,
'an epoch-making book'. Epoch-making! And have
we read it? And all those revolutions – have we
heard about them? And that was only up to 1930,

there's another forty years to go! And my God!
What shall we do?

ACT TWO SCENE ONE

SIMONE I'd like to do just that: die, go away and die. Creep
into the river or the stones on the street. Give me a
reason why not to, Roland.

You know what defeats me? My capacity for
nostalgia. I can project myself forward twenty years
from now and feel myself regretting what I've
not done today. That's what makes the present so
oppressive; it's bad enough aching for the years
gone by and suffering today's mess, but somehow I
manage to suffer tomorrow's reproach also, before
it comes. And it all defeats me. (*Beat.*) Just walk
out, away. Do it now. I'd get such peace. (*Pause.*)
Give me a reason why not, Roland… Never mind
whether I've been drinking. Give me a reason why I
shouldn't do it now, get up and walk away and never
come back. You can't, can you?… You can't give me
a reason, can you?…

You don't know what it's like to talk and not be
heard; to offer and not be taken; to be full and not
needed. There's not a creature needs me, not one
single one. They'll use me, drink with me, tolerate
my company, but not need – not really need me.
I feel so useless and rejected, so dismissed. You've
never known that, have you? God's chosen ones
you lot are, but not me. Look at my face. Long and
Gothic you say, you like telling me that, flirting
with the past. And my eyes, full of pleading.
Who can look at them? Full of pleas and sighs
and expectations – watery, dog-like; and long
limbs – drooping over this chair, like a wet doll,
awkward, embarrassing, waiting for crumbs; and
they all know it, and they retreat. I don't blame
them. Who can blame them? And I want to creep

away, just pick myself up and go and not come back.
I'd love that, I'd so love that.

ACT TWO SCENE TWO

MACEY   I can't sleep in this house; you're whimpering all
night and the others keep moving about. What the
hell good do you think you're doing there, Roland,
with all those cuts exposed? Put something over you,
you bloody child, you.

You're weird, all of you. And unnatural. Esther was
the only healthy one of the lot of you. Just let the
press get pictures of you all now. That'd be a scoop.
'The Trend-makers.' Huh! The habit of discontent
was all your lot ever created. Making the young feel
that the world belonged only to them. Real little
class terrorists you were, intimidating everyone over
the age of twenty-five with your swinging this and
your swinging that. You never thought you'd grow
old or die. Even the politicians and the poets were
frightened of you, you screamed so loudly about
your squalid backgrounds. Here, let me help you.
Look at you. They'll fester, those cuts. You must be
racked with pain. And put a pullover on, it's cold.

Wanders miserably round the room.

This room is festering. With gloom. Restless bloody
house.

Stops in front of MANFRED's model.*

Questions! Suddenly everyone's full of little
heavyweight questions. 'Who do you hate? Who
do you love? Why are you a manager?' Who asks
questions at my age? I know why I'm a manager,
what good does it do me?

Because each morning I wake up knowing that I
don't love the woman at my side, and haven't done
so for the last fifteen years –

---

* A recreation of the DNA module.

That defeats me that does, that really does defeat me.
No love – no appetites, for anything. Even before the
day begins I'm done.

But, I've managed. A good father taught me
discipline so I managed. Why, I asked myself,
why *exactly* did I resent her? Very important to
know. She's not a bad woman, very good in fact,
even wise – about simple things – loyal, sense of
humour – everyone loves her – except me; so
why? You know why? Because *I* had the capacity
to grow and *she* didn't. She grew, true, but, one day
she stopped and I went on. Simple! Not a reason
for resentment, you'd say – such a strong emotion,
resentment. True. But what I had to force myself to
accept was that she was a reflection of *me*: I chose
her. At one time in my life my entire capacity to
love had focused on her. And I had to ask myself,
'Could I have been capable of such small needs?' So
I resent her because she makes me despise myself.
She reminds me, every day, that at one time in my
life I'd wanted such small things.

But the next discipline was really hard; you listening,
Roland? Really hard! It was to avoid building up
those little heavyweight philosophies about man and
the world out of my own personal disappointments;
to avoid confusing self-hatred with hatred of all men;
to face the fact that though I'd failed, others hadn't.
There! Two disciplines! Two honest confessions!
But who's satisfied? No one is – are they? Because
they're no good really, those little bits of honest
confession. What am I supposed to do with them,
tell me what?

From *The Old Ones*

Synopsis:

The 'old ones' are Sarah; her two brothers, Boomy – the pessimist, Manny – the optimist; Manny's wife, Gerda, and Sarah's eccentric friends Teressa, Millie and Jack.

Manny and Boomy constantly quarrel.

The young ones are Rosa, Sarah's daughter; Rudi, Sarah's nephew; Martin, Boomy's son.

Set against scenes of old age, the play begins with preparations for the Jewish festival of Succoth, which no one knows quite how to put together, and ends with everyone gathered for the festival's meal.

The Old Ones *plays out the conflict between the optimistic and pessimistic spirit.*

THREE SPEECHES OF TERESSA

ACT ONE SCENE THREE

> *TERESSA's dishevelled attic living room. She's in her petticoat. A roll of toilet paper in her hand. She hoists her petticoat and wraps toilet paper round her middle.*

TERESSA You never know when you may need what.

> *Puts on a record of Beethoven's* Streichquartett *Op. 131, slips on her dress, moves to a mirror to adjust her hair, and heavily makes up her face. Surveys herself before mirror at which she constantly talks in a deeply Slavonic accent.*

All dressed up and nowhere to go. (*Pause.*) It's not funny, darling. If I wasn't an educated woman I'd understand, but I'm educated! A reader of books! A translator!

*She idly reaches for a piece of paper and reads from
it.*

'Wanda Wilczynski was born in 1857 in the market
town of Lashkowitz in Poland. To this town my
father went in terror of his life to sell his goods'

Corrects a mistake and becomes involved.

'and he brought back news of this strange poetess
whom everyone thought was mad. My father's
passion became mine and for this reason I have
felt it a duty to undertake the translation of her
poetry into this the most harmonious of languages'
'Harmonious'? That's a way to describe the English
language? 'Lyrical'. A better word.

*She scribbles the alterations but it's a casual stab at
work.*

Ach! Books! Thoughts! (*Stops record.*) If they live
in your head and you can't use them – useless!
Mocking! Fifteen years I've been translating you,
Wanda my darling. (*Moves again to mirror.*) Look
at my face. When did you last see a face that
said *so* much. It's all there, Teressa, full of lines,
and I can tell you which line is which. (*Pointing.*)
Disappointment, bitterness, self-hatred, heart-ache,
fear. Sour – all sour, my darling.

She turns away unhappily; then, defiantly.

I want to look beautiful!

*Shrugs. Moves to cut a slice of bread; eats it with a
lump of cheese, indifferently. Full mouth.*

Silly woman! Silly, silly woman, Teressa. (*Pause.*)
What's silly about wanting to be beautiful again?
Vanity? I've had my children, I've had my
heartache, now I want to look in a mirror and get
pleasure. I tell you, with that kind of pleasure I'd be
so generous, so generous and calm and dignified.
Sweetness, darling, there's such a sweetness in
beauty. Oh dear. Oh dear, dear me. (*Pushes away
food.*) Who can eat?

She picks up papers again.

'Her life was a tragedy. At the age of thirteen she was
sent to a sanatorium where it was thought to cure
her of tuberculosis. One day her parents received
a telegram; the postmaster had been ill and a boy
had been taken on for the day to deliver the mail.
Telegrams being unusual in small Polish towns the
mother tore it open without checking the envelope' –

*But she knows it all by heart and has no need to refer
to her notes –*

'the boy had taken it to the wrong address. It had
been meant for the apartment next door and by
strange ill-fortune the telegram read, 'Come at once
your child is very ill.' The child next door had been
staying with relatives and died without seeing its
parents. Wanda's parents packed at once but their
speeding carriage was involved in an accident that
proved fatal. These events hung like an accusative
hand of God over her life.'

What a life! And no one cared then and no one cares
now. Not about your poetry nor my translations.

ACT ONE SCENE ELEVEN

*TERESSA's room. She sits amid the chaos of her table,
working on her translations. A record of Beethoven's*
Streichquartett *Op.131.*

TERESSA   (*Reading from a sheet.*)

> For oh the wind like hammers hound
> And mock my life with warning sound;
> Those winds who for all others sing
> Prepare for me an inevitable ending.

'Prepare for me' or 'prepare me for'? There's a
difference. Or is there? Problems! (*Takes off record.*)
Always the same question: should I translate the
exact words or the exact meaning? The exact words

would be: '*The winds sing for everyone else but I am to be prepared for they whisper 'dying, dying'.'* The sense is poetic but the words aren't. Or are they? What about: (*Writing.*)

> Those winds who for all others sing
> Whisper to me of dying dying.

But then you lose her intention to show how the winds of life are preparing her for what she believes is the inevitable retribution of death. She feels guilty for her parent's death and she sees all life as her trial. Suppose we say:

> Those winds who for all others sing
> Prepare my death with whispering.

But then you see, Teressa darling, she repeats the words 'dying, dying' so that it also *sounds* like the wind. You'll lose all that. Well, something is always lost in translation I suppose. I wonder, would it matter if I made it a verse of five lines instead of four?

> Prepare me for my death
> With their whispering whispering.

So:

> For Oh the winds like hammers hound
> And mock my life with warning sound;
> Those winds who for all others sing
> Prepare me for my death
> With their whispering whispering.

God knows! Enough now. You've been working on that verse for two months now. Leave it alone. Come back to it next week.

Pushes paper aside and puts on the record again.

Now what should I do?

ACT TWO SCENE TWO

TERESSA's flat.

TERESSA   Perhaps if I do physical things I won't feel so lonely.

She pulls clothes from here and there, stuffing them away, attempting to create order.

Work, they say. Keep your body working! As if growing old you can do all the things you could when you were young.

Bending, she strains herself.

Aaah! Work, they say. Give me a new body – I'll work.

From a cupboard lined with medicine bottles she extracts a pill.

So! And that's for my lumbago. And what shall I take for the pain behind my ears, and my weak bladder, and my coughing fits and the pain in my chest and my fear? Fear! Who's got pills against fear?

On the table are a box of dominoes. She builds with them.

You know, darling, when a person *really* feels lonely? Not when they're alone and no one comes to see them – in such a case you can go out to people, even if they don't ask. No, it's when they don't have in their heart one little bit of a wish themselves to see other people. It's *not* having appetites for contact, that! That, my darling, makes for real loneliness. You, you're lucky, you're *not* lonely, you *want* contact. But who? That's your problem. And where? And when? (*Beat.*) And why? I always forget why. Such a memory! My memory is so bad that when I went to a psychiatrist to get it seen to I'd forgotten why I came. (*Pause.*) No! That's not true. It's funny but it's not true. Who can afford a psychiatrist? Jokes! Even jokes I have to tell myself, and *that's* not funny, darling. My poor darling.

**THE THIRD OF THREE CONFRONTATIONAL SPEECHES
FROM ROSA**

ACT TWO SCENE EIGHT

ROSA is a careers advisory officer.

*She's addressing a rowdy group of school leavers from
a tough neighbourhood. She is determined to control
them and does.*

ROSA   I'm here once and once only. And when I'm gone
I'll not care one bit about any of you but *you're* going
to care about and remember me.

You, each one of you, are nothing in this society.
Nothing! You are poor, used, nothings who will
mostly end up unhappy, frustrated and thoroughly
defeated. You *think* you're in control, that no one
can shove you around, that you're God almighty
free Englishmen but you're not. You can bash each
other and pinch sweets and knock old women on the
head but the great world goes on and ignores you or
knows and cares little for you just as you boast that
you know and care little for it. What, what is there
you can do? Can you take a yacht round the world?
Can you fly to wherever you want? Can you speak
another language, split an atom, transplant a heart,
live where you like, climb a mountain? You won't
even find the job you want, most of you. So get that
straight, firm, in your heads. It's a big world in which
control rests with other people, not *you*. *Not* you.

Good. You're listening. It makes a change. I don't
say any of these things happily. Do you think I
like how we're forced to live with each other? But
someone must warn you. Who knows, one of you
might even listen. One of you might rise to the
challenge and have done with his tiny ambitions of
petty kingships and turn in on himself and find his
real strengths. And it will *only* be one of you – the

rest will end up on the scrap heap of dead-end jobs with dead-eyed wives.

You hate me, don't you? I can see from your eyes and clenched mouths that you hate every part of me; the sound of my voice, what I say, the way I dress, the life you imagine I lead. I'm sorry about that. Hate is a sterile emotion. Useless! It'll take you round in circles while others go straight for what they want. Still, I suppose that's the diet most of you will live with from now on. Hate. Sad. BUT HERE! Here is a book. Books! Take them. Use them. Other men may build an alien world out there you never dreamed of. (*Urgent not strident.*) Defend yourself! Books! Centuries of other people's knowledge, experience. Add it to yours, measure it with yours. They're your only key to freedom and happiness. Books! (*Forlorn, weary, without hope for them.*) There is no other. I promise you. There – is – no – other!

ACT ONE SCENE FIVE

> *RUDI, SARAH's nephew, tall, wild-eyed and bearded; a compulsive talker of half-finished, disjointed thoughts, constantly accompanied by gestures. He is setting up an automatic slide projector from which will be projected, throughout his talking and eating, slides of his gaudily coloured, tortured, primitive-type paintings.*

RUDI A projector! Watch! Automatic and – no touching.

> *Switches off room light, switches on machine; we receive the first shock of his 'work'. Satisfied, he sits to eat.*

There! Photographs! You don't have photographs? No one believes you. Saves a lot of talking, explaining. Like this you show them, they can see, it's your work, your name. I get tired talking; lose breath, waste time, you know what I mean? You want to see some of the paintings? There's one in Hackney library and half a dozen in a new Israeli

restaurant, Stoke Newington end of Northwold
Road. Open ten in the morning till one, two, maybe
three in the morning, for three weeks. But I'm not
forcing you to go to not go you please yourself. Who
can force people? Force people you make enemies,
they get annoyed, they start lying – who can be
bothered? People always have excuses why they
can't go – they're busy, they've got appointments,
they're ill – I never knew people could be ill so
many times. You got commitments? I understand.
What can I tell you? That you're my aunt? That you
must go because you're family? Family is no reason.
You please yourself. You go because you *want* to go,
you're interested. You know what I mean? It won't
stop me. Nothing stops me. I go on because I know
if you don't go on for yourself you've had it; with
jealousy from this one from that one, you wouldn't
believe people can be so jealous, in every place, over
everything, one person watching you, another one
frightened in case you get more marks than them,
you know what I mean? Like this I paint and I keep
track where the paintings go. No one lets their work
go somewhere without them knowing, you can be
swindled, but me? I got photographs, with my name,
on both sides, and it's proof and one day they'll sell
and I'll earn money enough to take no notice of
the lot of them. And they want me, you know that?
To give my paintings. They chase me, write to me,
the librarian, to bring, to hang. Because people,
you know, they don't like reality, they hate reality,
they're frightened. That's why there's all these goings
on with revolutions and riots and violence.

But it costs money – for paints, for hardboard,
for framing. Me. I don't give them to frame any
more, I do my own the way I want them because
one painting I gave and I said I wanted it in ten
days' time and the girl wrote it down 'ten days' for
Saturday but I went and nothing was done. 'The
boys didn't know,' she said. They didn't know! They

didn't care! They didn't want to do any work, just
to get paid while they flirt around, so it wasn't done
and I took it away because who can wait while they
mess things up for you? Everyone's busy messing
things up for you. I could tell you stories. In every
business. Twisting and dishonesty. One bloke says to
me 'Take one of your paintings down and pretend
you sold it, fool the people.' But who can remember
such things? This story, that story – how long can
you go on doing that before you get found out – you
know what I mean? Me, I can't work that way.

…The other day I walked in the street and I found
a wallet so I picked it up and I could see people
watching me, waiting to see if I was gonna put it
in my pocket. But I counted the notes, the pound
notes and the pennies and all the receipts – packed
with receipts, you could see she did the football
pools – and I took it to the police station and there
there was forms, forms, you should see the forms,
and every penny was counted and noted down and
they told me if there was no claim in fourteen days
they'd write to me. But she claimed and I got the
letter with inside a postal order for ten shillings, and
it was worth everything to me, more than all the
values…

Who understands art?… People listen to other
people, no one comes to see the work and then they
want you to explain: 'what does it mean?'… What
does it mean!… They don't *know* what it means?…
They can't *see* what it means?… It means what I
understand!…

You know what I don't like doing? Portraits! A man
can only show one kind of face when he's made to
sit and think: sadness… One day the Kosher butcher
asks me to paint Dayan… Why Dayan?… 'Paint
Dayan please, it's a Jewish neighbourhood!'… So I
said, 'How can I paint Dayan? I don't know him!'…
'From a newspaper,' they said… A newspaper!…
'Give me a real live photograph,' I said, 'maybe I

can do something.'... The man in the restaurant asks
me to paint his sign – I don't mind that I'm an artist
and he asks me to paint his sign, but when it's only
half done he says he can't get a ladder to finish the
job. He *says*... But maybe it's not true... Maybe he
doesn't want to *pay* me... And maybe I won't ask to
be paid... But all of a sudden he can't get a ladder...
So, the sign's only half done...

I tell you, two things I don't do: I don't jump into
other people's business and I don't jump into other
people's fights. Who knows what it's all about,
you get caught up, *you're* the good one, and *you* get
murdered! By mistake!

ACT ONE SCENE FOUTEEN

> *BOOMY's room, filled with books and the scattered
> parts of a child's large computer and a semi-dismantled
> TV. BOOMY is helping his sister-in-law, GERDA, to
> make his bed.*

BOOMY I was eight when our father brought us over...
Did you know our father was rich?... He was rich
and he was careful. (*Fiddles with TV set.*) Before
leaving Lithuania he converted his money into
diamonds and gave them to a Gentile friend to
take to Amsterdam; and from there, every year,
his friend brought a few in for him. And slowly
he built up a business in Black Lion Yard off the
Whitechapel Road. One day – a robbery! An
ordinary common-or-garden robbery, and our
father, bless him, for all that he was wise and
careful, was not insured. Still, it was not the end of
the world. There was one last bag expected from
Amsterdam and those, our father said, were for
us to pay for our education. He was a frugal man,
needed very little – his sons would provide. And
to Manny, because he came first, he gave the little
bag of diamonds... Did you know Manny was one
of the first members of the Communist Party?... A

founder member! And you know what happened…
No, he did not give them to Party funds… I knew
you'd think that. And so would every sane-minded
person have thought it; and if he'd done that I think
I'd have understood better – I might even have
been proud. But no, that's not what happened.
One day he says to me – I was sixteen at the time,
the father dead, school finished, we were planning
University – and Manny says to me: 'Boomy, come
for a walk, let's see London, how much of London
do we know?' So we walked, through Spitalfields
to Liverpool Street, down through the City to
Mansion House and out along the Embankment to
Westminster. What a walk that was, exhilarating!
And we stood on the bridge and talked and talked
about the future. How I was going to study medicine
and he was going to study economics, perhaps
go into Parliament – young men's talk, brave,
happy. You ever stood on that bridge and looked
at London? Wordsworth wrote a poem from it, the
river bends, a wide sweep, you can look up you
can look down – beautiful! (*Pause.*) And we talked.
(*Pause.*) And suddenly Manny says: 'But Boomy,'
he says, 'Everything we do must come from our
own hands. You agree?' And of course I agree, 'cos
I thought he was only talking about the efforts we
would have to make in our studies. 'Good,' he says,
and he embraces me and we cry and before I know
it he's thrown the bag of diamonds into the river.
(*Pause.*) You're paralysed, aren't you, Gerda? Can
you imagine what *I* felt? I nearly choked him on the
spot. 'Little lunatic,' I yelled at him, 'lunatic!' And
he kept saying 'but you agreed, you agreed' until I
had to run away and he kept shouting after me, 'you
agreed!' Agreed!

   Long silence.

I'm not very good at being old. Some people are like
that; only a certain period in their life suits them.
Some are lovely children and rotten adults. Me, I

was good at being young, not because I enjoyed
it so much – I couldn't stop being bitter – but
because I had strength, I could fight. That's my
weakness, I can't bear being defenceless. You know
things? Defence! You got a profession? Defence!
You're articulate? Defence! Instead? Tailors. Little
schneiders. And now look at me, playing with
TV sets in order to start understanding things.
Now! Sixty-eight years old. Like a senile Doctor
Faustus. You noticed that about our family? Look
at our nieces and nephews: Rosa, trying to knock
awareness into young people; Rudi, all his savings
on night classes, psychiatry, engineering, singing
and now – a painter. Dabbling! My brother has
made of me, of our children, of himself – a dabbler.
Even Martin, my son. A revolutionary! From love?
No! From hate. Hatred of me. One thing leads to
another.

ACT TWO SCENE FOUR

*MILLIE's flat. She gazes, as always, out of the
window.*

MILLIE My daughters were evacuated to Wales, you know.
In the war. Five daughters I had. My poor husband!
No son! And three were big. Big girls – worked
in armaments. But the youngest? A place called
Tredegar, in a little stone cottage, no electricity,
no water, no nothing. Miles from anywhere. My
poor children. And this woman – you talk about
madness? – this woman made them do strange
things every night. One night combing her hair,
another night rubbing her back, then washing
her feet – funny woman. Who knows where your
children go in war time, eh? And *she* ended up in
a home. My daughter told me. She went back one
day and found her, in a room, padded, her hair
sticking out like a tree, and my daughter said, 'You

remember me?' And she did. For a second. She
called her name, Becky, and then she forgot.

Strange, yes? The whole place was strange. In
the school the teacher used to tell them 'Because
you're Jewish your nose will get longer and horns
will come out of your head!' My poor girls. They
believed him. Did you ever see? Horns! And each
night they used to look in the mirror and it was true.
They were growing girls and their noses got bigger!
And all the time they were waiting for the horns.
And all the time this woman, this mad woman,
kept saying 'Maybe your horns won't grow. Maybe
because you're in Wales they won't grow!' But the
teacher kept saying 'They must! They must!' Is that
a teacher I ask you? And one day they came home
for a holiday and my husband, God rest him, could
see they were unhappy so he asks them 'What's the
matter?' And they told him and he says 'Silly girls.
Look at me, your father, have *I* got horns?' And they
looked and he was right, they could see, no horns!

ACT TWO SCENE NINE

The Succoth dinner.

BOOMY Violence! Violence... Everyone's talking about
violence – a big mystery! What causes it! Whisper,
whisper, whisper, pssssss! Why don't they ask me?
Ask me, *I'll* tell them... They've never heard of
cultural intimidation? I'm not of course referring
to your so-called 'magnificent primitive working
man' – we all know nothing can intimidate him.
I'm referring to the men of *real* inferiority, men
who suspect their own stupidity. That's where
violence comes from. The anger of self-knowledge.
Self-knowledge that he's a pig and then – everything
intimidates him: a tone of voice, a way of dressing,
a passion for literature, a passion for music, for
anything! He hates it! One little speck of colour
on a man's personality unleashes such venom, *such*

venom… Money! Money! Don't tell me he hasn't
enough money. Money he has, and security and
a good job and a house and a car – everything.
Not riches, I'm not talking about riches, but like
us – enough. And still, and yet, his whole body,
every corpuscle in his thick blood is on fire and alive
to the slightest deviation from what *he* is. Can't bear
it! Grrrr! Hit it! Smash it! He'll show who's superior
and who's not. Wham! And there it is, all round him,
the intimidation – bookshops, television, flamboyant
actresses, cabinet ministers who went to university,
protesting students with long hair, trade union
leaders with big cars, black leaders with clenched
fists, pop singers, Hippies, Yippies, Queers, Yids!
'Know thyself!' everyone says. 'Unto thine own self
be true!' What's that for advice? We *know* ourselves.
Only too bloody true we know ourselves. That's the
trouble. We know ourselves too well. Grrrr! Can't
bear it!

And there they are, the intimidated, squirming in
their factories and shops, missing it all. The adverts
tell them! Missing it and hating it and hating
themselves for missing it. Trapped! All over the
place, in little black holes, trapped! Grrrr! Who can
I smash? Whose fault is it? Someone's got to suffer
as well as me. Wham! Nigger, Jew, Artist, Student!
Lynch 'em! Send 'em back! Bring back the gallows,
the whip, anything. I-hate-them! I-hate-me! Hate!
Grrrr! (*Beat.*) Violence? They want to know about
violence? Me! Ask me.

From *Love Letters On Blue Paper*

Synopsis:

Victor, a retired Yorkshire trade union leader is dying of leukaemia. He doesn't want to tell his wife, Sonia; instead he calls to his bedside the young Maurice Stapleton, Professor of Art, his protégé, with whom he talks about a book on art that he's writing, and in whom he confides attempting to confront 'the big questions' before dying.

Sonia writes letters to him with neither beginnings nor endings, posts them at the bottom of the road, and delivers them to him in the mornings with his other mail. Neither of them talk about the letters.

The letters begin as simple recollections and end as passionate declarations. Through them she reveals a love she was unable to express and, in recalling their glorious life together, prepares him for death.

FIVE SPEECHES OF VICTOR

VICTOR'S FIRST SPEECH

> *VICTOR's bedside. He's talking to MAURICE.*

Maurice don't bumble! I'm dying! It's myeloid leukaemia! I waited three years for these last months and they've come and that's that. Now, let me talk. (*Pause to gather strength.*) Oh, I'm frightened. No doubt about that. And bitter. Look at that sun, listen to those sounds, look at those books. Who'd want to leave all that? (*Picks up a newspaper.*) Despite all this. (*Reads.*) 'Allegations of torture to prisoners of war in North Vietnam.' Never stops does it? 'Man batters child to death. Youths batter old man to death. Quarter of London's homes without baths and heating. Sectarian killings in Belfast. Famine in India…'

> *He said it all in one breath which makes him cough and his irritation increase.*

(*Coughing.*) Still! Still, still, still! After what we did. All we did! (*Long pause.*) And yet – I don't want to leave any of it. I'd live with it all – just so long as I live. (*Pause.*) Retired me from the union just in time didn't they, eh?

> *VICTOR gets out of bed. MAURICE attempts to help. He refuses it. Puts on dressing gown. Begins talking. While talking he takes a medicine, and potters, reshuffling stacked canvases, replacing a bust. Rearranging the order of things.*

I'll tell you a story. Told me by the head of one of the largest unions in West Germany. Fantastic fellow he were, still is, I suppose. God knows! Lose touch with them. You share a special conference or something together, bosom pals, console each other through dreary affairs – and you know we used to get some boring old sods at those conferences, self-righteous little functionaries they were – but not Heuder. Wolfgang Heuder. Very vivid *he* was. Dragged into the Wehrmacht when he was fifteen, last months of the war. I was probably chasing him in one of my tanks! It was him told me this story.

Seems their regiment picked up a deserter, some poor scrawny old man who'd been out of the war because of flat feet or asthma or something but now they were taking in anyone who could hold a rifle. *He'd* no appetite for the glorious Third Reich right from the start so he'd precious little urgency to die for it in its last gasps. Who would? And off he scarpered. *He* could smell defeat. But – he'd no energy. Food supplies low, foot-sore, wheezing – he was caught, court-martialled, and sentenced to a firing squad. That depressed everyone it seemed. No one had stomach for it, not even the regiment commander. But he was an old soak, duty was duty, regulations was regulations. There had to be a trial, it had to be a fair trial, there had to be a sentence, it had to be carried out. Victims of law and order when all law and bloody order were crumbling round them. Madness, eh?

Still, the commander was an honourable man and he asked the prisoner if he had any last wishes. You know what the poor bugger asked for? A plate of barley soup! Wanted to eat before dying. To go off on a full stomach as it were. It were staple fare and there were some left to be heated up in the kitchens so they give it him. What he'd asked for. A plate of barley soup!... And when it were finished, now listen to this, when it were finished he asked for another plate! That were unprecedented but, nothing in the rules to say a condemned man couldn't have as much of his last request as he wanted, and rules were rules! So, another plate was called for and the man ate it slowly. And when he'd finished, yes, he asked for another plate and this time they had to wait while it was being made because they'd run out of the previous night's left-overs. And he ate! And he ate, and he ate, and he ate! Barley soup! More'n he wanted, more'n he could take. Anything, so long as it delayed the moment of his death. And you know what happened? The Russians came. The sentence couldn't be carried out. Everyone fled. He lived! He couldn't have known he'd live but some instinct kept him eating. Eating to stay alive! Ha! Simple.

I've given you a real shock haven't I, lad? Terrible. (*Cheerfully.*) Look at those pillows. Fresh every day. She changes them. Every day. Believe it or not I get into fresh sheets every night. I tell her there's no need but she takes no notice. 'You spent good money on a washing machine' she says, 'I'll use it then!' Love it, of course. (*Pause.*) I'm sorry, lad, you look quite pale. Daft bugger, me.

VICTOR'S SECOND SPEECH

It began about three years ago. In the middle
of a strike. I began to suffer from headaches
and dizziness… The hospital workers'
strike – remember? Daft government policies.
What a time that was. All-night discussions about
compromise, open-air gatherings up and down the
country – the lot! So, blood pressure, I thought, and
went for a check-up. Nothing! Blood pressure was
high but not pathological. My general condition was
good. Next day, a phone call. Specialist's assistant.
Would I go and see them. Something's cropped up.
When I saw the specialist the next day he told me:
high white corpuscle count. Just like that! Almost
angrily, as though I were to blame. Like being told
I'd an overdraft. And then, well, I was – curious.
I was curious about what I was going through.
Curious, you know, like a bystander.

It were strange. I'd no sense of shock or fear, no
sweating or increased pulse. Just a great slowing
down of time. Everything – in slow motion. No,
don't ask me to be logical about it. I only know what
happened, in this order, as I'm telling you. And
then, into this slow motion, came this great increase
of – don't laugh, it's difficult for me to say it, but
this – great increase of love. I didn't feel it. It wasn't
that. But I had, suddenly, a better *sense* of it. And
then, relief. I was aware of how tired life had made
me, how tired I was of myself and how, now, now
I could be held responsible for nothing more. Ever
again.

Sonia asked what it were and I told her it were the
strike. But she'd seen me in strike times before so I
had to tell her half the truth, that I'd seen a doctor
and that he'd told me to go easy because of high
blood pressure. Anyway, 'we're not certain' the
specialist said, 'but all the evidence points to myeloid
leukaemia.' I knew the implications of that of course,

but I wanted to hear it spelt out. 'Fifty per cent of the people in your condition live for three years' he said, 'of the other fifty per cent many live for five, some for ten. A few have been known to live for twenty but that's rare. Some have died within the year but that's just as rare. You have my answer.'

Ha! I had his answer all right. But, as you said, they can be wrong. It's been known. So I saw someone else. And what a bastard he turned out to be. A diehard old Tory who'd obviously always hated my guts. When I asked him for a prognosis he said: 'If you've got some papers that need signing you can leave them, but if you've got a fortune to make I'd start making it right now.' I ignored all that and just asked about the possibility of cure or spontaneous recovery. And you know what he said? 'Cure is a dirty word!' A right bastard he were. It was from my own doctor, my own old GP that I managed to find a little comfort. I remember he embraced me first and then said: 'Vic, you aren't *worried* about it are you? *You're* not going to die of leukaemia. A heart attack, maybe, a plane crash, anything! But not leukaemia. Myeloid leukaemia,' he said, 'for a person in your condition and at your age is a benign ailment. Eat very well. Go to bed early. Get up a bit later. Avoid infections. Keep outdoors as much as possible, and don't tell anybody, it only creates the wrong atmosphere.' Great man, that. Restored my sanity. So, there it is. I belonged to the fifty per cent who last three years. My time's up. The Myleran and Purinethol are having less and less effect. I'm up and I'm down. I recover but I recover more slowly. It still just looks like high blood pressure to Sonia but *I* know. I *know* what's happening.

VICTOR'S THIRD SPEECH

Can't bear heavy skies. Sooner imagine it was
night-time than face morbid bloody clouds. Look
at those stunned starched overfed cushions. They
reproduce themselves when I'm not looking.
(*Beat.*) Well? My notes, for my book. (*Beat.*) A
mess aren't they? Confused. Gibberish. A mess.
(*Beat.*) When I wrote all that down I thought it was
the beginning of a profound enquiry that would
unravel why everyone concludes it's a rotten life.
Have you noticed that? Everyone says it's a rotten
life. 'People are rotten!' Life, literature – all filled
with characters whose experience of the world is
depressing. So – who upsets them? Speak to the man
who they say has upset them and you find *he* also
thinks the world is a rotten place and that people are
rotten. And who's upset *him*? Where does it begin?
Everyone knows it's a terrible life only it never
seems possible to lay your finger on the culprit, the
cause. I know people have got answers – religious,
political, philosophic. But at the end of everyone's
life, whether he's a revolutionary leader, a dictator,
a pope, a millionaire – a worker, a prime minister, a
socialist citizen, a citizen of the west – a great artist, a
great scientist, a great philosopher – for all of them!
Terrible life! By the end of it they're all weary and
disillusioned and dispirited. I mean listen to Ruskin.
(*Reaches for a book.*) Who could want to have achieved
more? But was *he* happy? Listen. (*Reads.*)

'I forget, now, what I meant by "liberty" in this
passage; but I often use the word in my first writings
in a good sense, thinking of Scott's moorland
rambles and the like. It is very wonderful to me,
now, to see what hopes I had once: but Turner was
alive then, and the sun used to shine, and the rivers
to sparkle.'

Too late, Maurice lad. Were a trade union leader too long. Should've given up at forty and started to study for me book then. But not now.

VICTOR'S FOURTH SPEECH

VICTOR is in hospital. MAURICE at his bedside.

I've started to imagine this other place. Supposing it did exist. Just supposing. What *could* it be like? I mean I can't even begin to imagine what it would be like visually. Where do you place it, this – after-life? And then I think: it's not a physical place, Victor, that's where you go wrong. It's a spiritual state, a state of awareness unconfined by a physical framework. Ha! And so I lie in there trying to project myself into 'a-spiritual-state-of-awareness-unconfined-by-a-physical-framework'! Ever tried to do that? Try it some day. And then I get angry and I say to myself: 'Darkness! Nothing! When you're dead that's it. Over! Done! If you want satisfaction, Victor lad, then look to your life, your political battles, the fights you fought for other men.' But who can do that for long, dwell on his past and go scratching for bits of victory? Eh? A smug man perhaps. But I'm not a smug man, Maurice, never was. So what's left? No after-life I can conceive of and no past to feel at peace with. And I go round and round in circles driving myself mad because even the very act of contemplating it, me! thinking about whether there's a heaven, another life, the very worrying about such things makes me feel guilty and shabby. '*You*, Victor? Worrying about where you're going? Frightened are you?' I taunt myself. 'Frightened? Poor, feeble-minded man, you. You who used to be so confident about it all beginning with birth and ending with death. You! Want a comfortable little heaven to go to now? Do you?' And I'm a merciless bugger you know. Really get to the heart of myself, where it hurts. Always

been like that. Have you ever thought about the
tone of voice your conscience has? Everyone's got a
conscience which talks to them in a different tone of
voice. Mine jeers. Very acidy.

VICTOR'S FIFTH SPEECH

Still from a hospital bed

It's going to be a long bloody job. Longer'n I
thought. Longer'n they told me in fact. (*Pause.*) You
typed my notes?

*First tries reading with his glasses. Then reaches for
an enormous magnifying glass.*

No good. It's no good. I'm going blind. Oh bloody
Christ! Maurice!

Long pause.

You don't believe in God, do you, professor? Right!
You can't. Nor can't I. But the ceasing forever of
all this (*Knocks angrily on his skull.*) – *that* doesn't
make sense either. (*Beat.*) Of course there are *some*
people to whom it makes ecstatic sense, but they're
a type, the put-downers I call them. Any bloody
opportunity they get, they enjoy putting men down.
They have a special tone of voice, the kind of voice
that rubs its hands together. 'Look at the ocean'
they cry, 'see what a little thing is man in all that
sea!' And when space rockets came they had a real
ball. 'Look at all those stars. How insignificant is
man now!' Instead of marvelling that man could
make it to the bloody moon they found it another
opportunity to put him down. And now there's those
stupid computers. Oh how they do love putting men
down because they can't store up facts mechanically.
But a computer's a poor thing compared to a brain
isn't it? I mean, bloody hell, I'm no scientist but even
I know that. Can't store a shred of what the brain
can. But on they go. The put-downers! Of which I
mercifully have never been one. So it doesn't make

sense. It just doesn't make sense. I *know* it's going
to happen and nothing's ever stopped it happening,
but it just doesn't make sense. It's so – so unjust. No
reason for it. I mean what have I done to have all
those bloody marvellous things taken away from
me? What? What, what, what for Christ's sake?
(*Pause.*) Daft bugger, me.

> *This next speech takes place some days later but can*
> *follow on. He's looking at the blood transfusion bottle*
> *at his bedside.*

Have to renew it every three hours. Stop the flow
and I die. Look at it! A bottle of someone else's
blood, just that red stuff in there to keep me able
to see you and talk and think – and remember and
reason. (*Shifts a little.*) Bloody bedsores. I've got a
rubber ring under my backside but it makes no odds.
Lying horizontal still stops the blood circulating.

This is it, Maurice, isn't it? Oh, don't protest, lad.
I don't think I mind now all that much. Like your
mother. I understand her. In fact, I've got back
me curiosity. You know what helped? I woke up
the other day and suddenly out of the blue no
connection with anything, I thought: Leonardo da
Vinci is dead. And that seemed reassuring. So I went
on: Mozart is dead. Socrates is dead. Shakespeare,
Buddha, Jesus, Gandhi, Marx, Keir Hardie – they're
all dead. And one day Sonia will die. And my son,
Graeme, he'll be dead, and my daughter Hilda, and
their son, Jake, and so will all the grandchildren.
And there seemed a great unity to it all. A great
simplicity. Comforting.

SONIA'S EIGHT LOVE LETTERS

1ST LETTER I was thinking the other day. I used never to be able
to call you 'darling'. Do you remember? When we
first met I was really plain. Plain-minded I mean, not
looking. I was pretty looking but I felt daft saying

'darling' and 'sweetheart' and those things. Took
about two years before I could bring myself to call
you any but your name. And I only ever gave in
because you bullied me. Got proper annoyed in fact.
You *made* me say the word, forced me. Remember?
I do. It was after we'd been to have tea with my
grandmother. A Sunday afternoon. One of those big
spreads. Everything thrown on the table, you know,
from home-made pickle onions to thick old crusty
rhubarb pies. And she was making her usual fuss of
me. Adored me she did and I did her too, and she
was teasing me and saying 'she's a little darling, *isn't*
she a little darling? She's *my* little darling.' And when
we walked home you turned on me and said 'She
can say the word why can't you?' 'What word?' I
asked. 'Darling!' you yelled. 'Go on, say it!' You *did*
look funny, your face all angry while your mouth
was saying words of loving. Didn't go together
somehow. '*Say darling*' you shouted at me and made
me giggle. And the more I giggled the more angry
you got. But you won, you made me say it. 'Darling!'
'Sweetheart Victor', 'dearest Victor', 'darling Victor',
'darling, darling' and 'my heart'. I was remembering.
Just today. For no reason. While I was outside
cleaning the windows.

2ND LETTER   You used to tease me about God. Soft brain I had
in them days. Could I help it though? My soft
brain, yes, but not my religiousness. That were
my upbringing. No one can be blamed for that,
though they do say the sins of the fathers should fall
upon the sons, but that's cruel and unreasonable.
Not that you were like that, you weren't cruel and
unreasonable no never I'm not saying that. But you
teased and you shouldn't have done because I was
badly hurt by it. You didn't know that I was, but I
was. Very badly hurt. To begin with. Then my brain
got hard. 'God is one man's invention to frighten
other men into being good' you said. 'But no one's
good if they're frightened.' That's what you said and

it sounded very reasonable to me. Besides, there was the war and all of them soldiers being gassed and slaughtered and then it happened to my brother Stan so I couldn't much believe in God. But I missed him. I don't mind telling you I missed God. Used to give me lovely pictures to think about. It was a long time before I knew what it was you gave me. Better. You know that don't you? After the teasing and tormenting my brain got harder and I grew proud of what I got to understand and how I could listen to you and your mates arguing and saving the world and make up my own mind. Did you *know* I grew? Couldn't talk or argue much or write but I grew from God to you. Became a woman. For a while at least.

3RD LETTER   The only time I ever swore was a night you got more than normal drunk and wept because things weren't going right in the union and you began complaining at me. You told me 'You don't care about me or my state or the fact that I'm losing me nerve and failing me mates, do you? And you haven't a care for rights nor conditions nor wages nor nothing.' Remember that? How you raged and wept and screamed. 'I'm going to pieces, I'm going to pieces and you don't care and you don't understand.' Very loud you were that night, my love, and I railed back 'Of course I care of course I understand but I won't give consolations to a man when he's filled with pity and shit. That's what you are' I said, 'you're filled with pity and shit.' Huh! The only time you wept and I swore, that was.

And that *was* a tense time. Very tense that was, my love. I'm laughing as I write it down. You looked so funny, so startled. I felt very bucked with myself to have startled you so. It was serious then but I confess now I giggled afterwards. Went away and giggled to myself. I'm laughing even as I write about it. Oh dear. Ha ha! 'Full of pity and shit!' I said. You forgot all about your going to pieces then. Aye. You were so shocked. Pity and shit! Ha! Ha!

4TH LETTER The lilac is dead. Don't ask me how but it's had a blight. Remember the lilac? We planted it forty-one years ago and uprooted it four times for four changes of house. It survived all those uprootings, and now… I'd be lost without my garden. It's not just a place I potter around in you know. I think you think it is. 'Thank God she's occupied' you say to yourself. I bet. No, it's a place where I think my best thoughts, my *only* thoughts in fact even though they don't amount to many. And where I touch all manner of things like earth and leaves, squashed worms and stones and colours and fresh air and smells and winds and clouds and rain and sunlight and – the cycle of things. *You* used to be like that, loving the cycle of things. It's you I got it from.

Remember how the lilac came? You brought it home one day and said we must start a garden. You'd got it from the old railway porter. It was a sucker and you told me, lilac cuttings were always suckers, from the roots not the branch. A thin thing it was with only a few wispery strands between living and dying. I didn't think it would take but you did and it started our garden off.

What about the arguments we had? We had our first rows over our first garden. What shape it should be, what should grow in it, which way it should face. You would insist the sun came up in one place while I knew darn well it came up in another. So what did we do? Daft buggers, we set the alarm to get up before sunrise. You were wrong of course. You've no idea how important it was to me to have been right about that. It was my first landmark. Gave me great confidence that did.

And as for the quarrels about what we should grow, well – I thought it would end our marriage. I wanted more veggies and you wanted more flowers. You said it wasn't a real saving to grow our own veggies, only an illusion. But you said, all right, we'll have more veggies only I had to keep accounts. You

made me work out what it cost in seed and labour
and I had to weigh all what grew and then check
it with the price in the markets and make a sum of
it all. And I did it too. Worked all hours figuring it
out. Mad people. But I loved it. Columns of figures
all very neat, and grand headings. Looked very
important. I got top marks at school for neatness.
Loved it. And was I proud. I *was* proud. Gave me
great pleasure and I was right. Again. It *did* pay
to grow our own veggies. That was my second
landmark. A huge garden. Planted everything in it
bar the sun. When you insisted I learned to drive
a car, that was a landmark. When you asked me to
show the Italian delegation around London without
you, that was a landmark. When you first went
abroad for a fortnight and I carried my affairs and
your affairs alone without you, that was a landmark.
When you first put your head between my legs, that
was a landmark...

5TH LETTER On the day we got married I thought you hated
me. I must tell you that, because it's the only
time I've ever seen hate in your eyes. What am I
doing marrying a man who hates me, I thought
to myself? You were so silent, so angry. But
afterwards – well – I didn't ever say but I used never
to be able to take my eyes off you. No one had ever
been so tender *and* certain. And you used to sing.
Once a visitor came from abroad I can't remember
where, France I think, and he said to me 'Good God,
there's someone who can still sing.' Our son sang
also. I remember we'd wake and find him standing
up in his cot looking down on us, not crying, not
murmuring, nor nothing, just patiently waiting for us
to wake up. And when we did he was the first thing
we looked at and he knew it and waited for it and
then gave us a slow smile and started to hum. Nearly
every morning was like that. You were daft about
our son. Wanted him to be a composer. You used to
play classical records in the bedroom while he was

asleep. 'It's best it sinks into him unconsciously' you said. Weird theories you had. You wouldn't ever *tell* him to think of music as a career, that would put him off, but if it went in...if it went in...

SONIA leaves off writing and reaches for the Shorter Oxford Dictionary.

Now what was that word he used? Began with an S. (*Flicks pages.*) P, Q, R, S. S! 'S' what? 'S' 'i'? 'Siderite' – a steel coloured stone. Well it wasn't that. 'Sibilate' – to hiss. It wasn't that either. What a lot of lovely words. 'Solatium' – a sum of money paid for injured feelings. 'Solazzi' – a stick of liquorice...Ah ha! Subliminal! That was it! Subliminally (*Turns back to letter.*) ...that would put him off, but if it went in subliminally...there! See what writing to you does for me?

Where was I? Music! There was one day, my God don't I remember that day, the children must have been about nine and eleven and you took us a climb on the peaks. Dangerous old route you took us. *You* were scared too. You won't remember it but you got us on to a tricky part where you had to go back and forwards across a gap four times in order to help me and the children, and you were sweating. The children thought it was great fun. They would. You would never let them be frightened of anything. Not always a good thing I thought. Still, I remember that trip for three reasons. The dangerous climb was one. The other was you letting out by accident that you'd had a girlfriend before me who'd climbed with you on that same walk. You blushed when you realised it had been let out. In fact I wasn't sure if you were talking about a girlfriend before me or after me... And the third thing was the song we sang at the top when we got there. We ate sandwiches and there was a big wind and you cried out like a madman 'we must sing against the wind, good for the lungs and the spirit.' So you taught us a round. The words were:

By the waters, the waters of Babylon
We lay down and wept and wept
For these I am.
Thee remember thee remember thee
remember
These I am

What did it mean? I never knew what it meant. Not
all this time. 'We wept for these I am.' What *are*
'these I am'? Do you think you got it wrong? We all
used to get songs wrong as children. I used to think
it was 'Good King Wences Last Looked Out' instead
of 'Good King Wenceslas Looked Out'. Perhaps it
should have been 'Thee zion.' Perhaps we should
have wept 'for thee Zion'. Or no – now I come to
think of it – you were probably right after all and we
wept because I am these things, we are these things,
all are these things.

6TH LETTER You took me and you shaped me and you gave me
form. Not a form I couldn't be but the form I was
meant to be. You needed only to be in the house and
I felt my life and the lives of the children I cherished
could never go wrong. It was so. They never did go
wrong. They have confidence and pity and daring in
them. And in me there are flowers. Blossoming all
the time. Explosions of colour and energy. You see it,
surely? Surely you see it? Or feel it? There's nothing
I couldn't do. In me is you. All you've given me. I've
been a white sheet, a large white canvas and you've
drawn the world upon me, given outline to what
was mysterious and frightening in me. Do you *know*
how proud I've been of you? Do you know I've felt
myself beautiful only because *you* chose me? Do you
know that I've shuddered with pleasure to think you
love me? You are my rock my hero my love. I feel
such strength. Do you know these things?

7TH LETTER Oh my beloved, my dearest dearest one. I have
adored you. Do you know that? That I am full of
you – do you? Know it? Know it? That I feel you

there as I've felt my children in me, your blood in
my blood, rivers of you, do you know it? Do you?
Do you? The sound of your voice, your judgements,
your praise, your love, your pity – all in me, do you
know it? My darling, oh my darling. Nothing has
been wrong for me and nothing will be. I will give
you my everything, cut from me my everything – all
my body's everything. To flow in you… What
nonsense do I write instead of just I love you and I
always have loved you? But I must catch up on too
much silence. So this nonsense, this silliness, this
too-much-writing-and-talking-and-shouting is all for
you because I can trust it all and anything to you.
Don't you know now what I feel? Can't you feel
what I feel, mad old woman that I am now? Can't
you understand I'd rip myself apart for you, oh my
beloved, oh my sweet sweet sweetest one. Why am I
so clumsy, never graceful as you deserved. Wretched
body, wretched heart, dull old mind. Not any part of
me good enough for you I know but oh I love you
love you love you oh my Victor Victor, love you,
Victor, love you, oh my Victor my heart.

8TH LETTER   There will be my darling one, I know it, a blinding
light a painful light when suddenly the lie will fall
away from truth. Everything will make its own and
lovely sense, trust me trust me. It won't be logical or
happy, this sense, but clear. Everything will become
clear. Trust me. Contradictions won't cease to be
contradictions, I don't say that, but nor will they
any longer confuse. I'm not promising all will seem
to have been good, but evil won't bewilder you as
it once did. Trust me, I adore you. And with this
blinding light will come an ending to all pain. The
body's pain the heart's pain the pain in your soul. All
in a second. Less than a second. Less than less than
a second. I'm sure of it. That's how it will be for us
all, I've always known it. No matter how it happens
to us. Accident, torture, suddenly at the top of our
energies, quietly in bed. There will come this flash,

this light of a colour we've never seen before. It's a glorious moment beloved. Even for the simpleton, even for him, his foolishness falls away just as from the madman his madness falls away. In the instant they know death so they know truth. In the blinding light of truth they know death. One and the same. I promise you, trust me, love O my love O my Victor O my heart.

From *The Journalists*

Synopsis:

Theme, set in the early 70s, is: 'the lilliputian mentality.'

The main action takes place in the open offices of The Sunday Newspaper.

The time span covers six days in six different weeks. Monday of the first week, Tuesday of the second week, etc. Two different periods of time are passing therefore, within which structure news events are discussed and personal lives played out.

The play is punctuated by three major interviews with Tory Cabinet Ministers conducted by Mary Mortimer, the central character, a tough journalist with her own column, who becomes obsessed to bring down a politician she suspects is a charlatan and inspiration behind The Angry Brigade. In the process she brings down one of her own children.

Mary's current assignment is to interview political leaders over a period of time in different settings – their office, their home, over a meal in a restaurant...

FIRST INTERVIEW – FROM ACT ONE PART ONE

> *MARY's first interview with Sir ROLAND SHAWCROSS, Minister for Social Services, in his office.*

SHAWCROSS And that, Miss Mortimer, is precisely what democracy is: a risky balancing act. The delicate arrangement of laws in a way that enables the state to conduct its affairs freely without impinging upon the reasonable freedom of the individual. Tilt it too much one way or the other and either side, state or individual, seizes up, unable to act to its fullest capacity...

Our first hour is nearly up. Tomorrow you're dining with us at home – it is tomorrow, I think? We can continue then. But for the moment I'd like to speak off the record. You've created a very unique reputation in journalism. Rightly and properly

you're investigating the minds and personalities
of men who shape policy. And you're doing it in
depth, in our offices, our homes, and on social
occasions. I'm surprised so many of us have agreed
and perhaps it will prove a mistake. We'll see. But
there are aspects of government which it's obviously
foolish of us to discuss in public no matter how
eager we are to be seen being open and frank. I'm
not evasive but, to be blunt, some of my thoughts
are so harsh they could be demoralising. Ah! you
will say, that is the truthful part of the man I'm after.
But I often wonder, how helpful *is* the truth? You're
right, the ordinary man must face the numb and
bureaucratic mind. Our best intentions are distorted
by such petty minds. But that can't really be my
concern, can it? I might then be forced to observe
that the petty mind is a product of a petty education.
Should I then go to complain to the Minister of
Education? He might then say education is only *part*
of the influence on a growing person – there's family
environment to be considered. Should he then
interfere in every man's home? No, no, no! Only
God knows where wisdom comes from, you can't
legislate for it. Government can only legislate for the
common good; the individual good is, I'm afraid, what
men must iron out among themselves. But I don't *act*
on those thoughts. My attempts on legislation are not
less excellent because I doubt the excellence of men
to interpret them. So, which truth will you tell? That
I aspire to perfection of the law? That I mistrust the
middle men who must exercise that law? Or will you
combine the two? The first is pompous, the second
abusive, the third confusing… No! Frankly I do not
think most people can cope with honesty…

We'll continue, we'll continue. I must leave.

Both go to the door which he holds open.

And it's not necessary to keep saying 'with respect',
Miss Mortimer. Do you enjoy saying it? Funny thing,

but people enjoy saying things like 'your honour'
'your Majesty' 'your highness' 'with respect'…

SECOND INTERVIEW – FROM ACT ONE PART TWO

*Lounge in the home of the Rt Hon GEORGE CARRON,
Minister for Science and Technology. He's a Northern
man, playing chess with MARY MORTIMER.*

CARRON I'm a bachelor, Miss Mortimer. If I'd been
married – nice cultured woman and all that – I
might be more interested in literature, film, plays.
But I'm not… So after three gruelling sessions with
this old man, ask away. I'll tell you what I mind and
don't mind. But art? Can't help you there. You'll
have to put me down as uncultured. Science and
politics, those are my passions… And chess, my only
addiction. Check.

Look, I'm an old man and, I'll confess, not a very
happy one. I began my career as a Labour politician
from a farm labourer's background and halfway
changed my politics to Tory – a man's driven by
the profit motive, plain and simple, I soon found
that out. But, it makes for a lonely life. To be
despised – not nice. You live with it but you never
get used to it. Still, that's not the point. What I'm
saying is that experience shaped me, not art. I didn't
change roads because of what I read in books, but
because of what I read in man. I'm tone deaf, colour
blind and get very impatient with the convenient
concoctions literary men make into novels. I saw a
play once and I thought to myself, yes, well, them
people behave like that 'cos they got good scripts
written for them. I prefer men who write their
own scripts. They do it in 'The House' and they
do it in the cabinet and they do it at international
conferences and that's real. Art shaping society? I
doubt it. Science, yes, not books. Still, I've got to
believe that haven't I? Minister for Science and
Technology and all that… You haven't moved out of

check yet… No, no children. My one regret. Watch
out for your queen…

Your editor wants to focus on the science versus
politics debate? Facile divisions. Journalese.
Look, the argument goes like this, I know it: there
develops, it is said, unnoticed by most of us, a whole
range of scientific discovery which creeps up behind
societies and suddenly – is there! And each time it
happens, the argument goes, then all the political
deliberations of decades are rendered useless and
we have to begin to formulate our opinions all
over again. Right? It's an attractive picture and
I can see why newspapers choose it as a popular
controversy – it's ripe for over-simplification!

But how accurate is it? Look at the period between
1900 and 1913, 'La Belle Époque' we call it.
Worldwide economic growth, prosperity, scientific
and technological advances, the lot! Science made
possible by politics, not in *conflict* with it. But look
what happened after 1913 – something neither
science nor political philosophy could account for:
an idiotic, soul-destroying world war! And the big
question to be asked is – who *should* account for it?
Newspapers can't. The answers are too complex,
so they oversimplify which is what you and your
newspaper are trying to do. Science versus politics!
Ha! A non-starter. Books! History! The interaction
of ideas – that's where you'll find your answers and
where I think you ought to guide your readers for
their answers…

Contradictions! Well, you've got to live with them
also. A Jewish MP once told me a story about an
old rabbi who was asked to settle a dispute between
two men. The first man tells his version and the
rabbi listens, thinks, and says: 'You know, you're
right.' Then the second man presents his side of the
argument and the rabbi listens, thinks, and says:
'You know, you're right.' At which the rabbi's pupil
who was standing by waiting for wisdom says: 'But

rabbi, first you said this man was right, then you said that man was right. How can that be?' And the rabbi listened, and thought, and said: 'You know what? You're also right.'

THIRD INTERVIEW – FROM ACT TWO PART THREE

An arbour in the grounds of the home of the Chancellor of the Exchequer, SIR REGINALD MACINTYRE. He is strolling up and down with MARY MORTIMER.

MACINTYRE   The final question? You won't be offended if I say 'thank God!' Three sessions is the longest I've ever given to any one journalist.

He listens.

Let me understand you. You are asking – how do I reconcile the needs of my own private standards of living with the needs of those working-people whose standards of living I, as Chancellor, must regulate?... Impertinent? Yes, I suppose I do find it that. (*Pause.*) Do you mind if I answer in an oblique way, without, I trust, being evasive?

It's a terrible problem, democracy. You see, if we could turn round and say all men who are dustmen are dustmen because of their inequality of opportunity then it would be easy. No problem. We would simply create equal opportunity. But it's not so, is it? Make *opportunity* equal and the inequality of their qualities soon becomes apparent. It's a cruel statement to make but, men are dustmen or lavatory attendants or machine minders or policemen because of intellectual limitations. There! Does that offend you? It used to offend me. Most unpalatable view of human beings, but all my encounters with them point to that fact. Even if we automate all sewage, everything, we're still confronted with the awful fact that some men *are* born with intellectual limitations. Now, what do we do? We can't talk of these things, it's taboo. We can't say in public 'some men are less intelligent than others' – though it *is* part of any discussion on democracy. So what *should* we do? Compensate their inadequacies with large pay packets? But what of the dustman? Because when he strikes for more pay he may not be asking to be paid for his ability or responsibilities but he *is* asking to be paid for doing *what other men don't want to do*, for what I think should be named 'the undesirability factor'. Isn't *that* a distinction? And a very intimidating distinction I may add. In democracies those who do our dirty work have us these days by, as they say, the short and curlies. Now, government must, you'll agree, remain in civilised hands. So, whose 'short and curlies' should civilised man hold on to without appearing to be so doing?

Does that also shock you? But ask yourself: don't you make a man feel simple by confronting him with problems beyond his intellect? Wouldn't it be civil, more kindly, more human *not* to discuss with a simple man what was beyond his intellect, or ask him to perform duties beyond his power? Surely you'd want me to *appear* to be his equal which I could only do by not frustrating or humiliating him in that way.

Yes, I know – what if my judgements of him are wrong? But what if all our judgements are wrong? Yours of me, mine of you – so? Do we cease making them? We are appointed because our judgements are more often right than wrong. That too is one of the risks of democracy, unless you can find me a man who can create a system – or a system which can create a man – whose judgement is right, all the time, about everything.

Do you find an answer shaping in all that? Am I making myself clear? You will, of course, let me see the typescript before going into print?

TWO SPEECHES FOR MARY MORTIMER

ACT ONE PART TWO

> *MARY MORTIMER's lounge. She has just fed her*
> *three children at a monthly 'family dinner'. Each*
> *has a different profession and all three are critical of*
> *what they think is their mother's pontificating weekly*
> *column 'Opinions'. The evening has, as usual, gone*
> *disastrously wrong.*

MARY I AM NOT BOURGEOIS! Bourgeois is a state of
mind, not of wealth... To hell with the classic sense.
Words acquire new meanings. Think! You have to
think about them. Your lot are so bloody mindless.

> *With forced calm and mounting distress.*

I loved and cared for my children, was that
bourgeois? That was natural, an old, old cycle tested
long before men began exploiting men. I gave you
a home to grow strong in, not to seclude you but to
help you face an insecure world, was that bourgeois?
Did I force you into professions you were miserable
with? Look at yourselves. Are you enfeebled,
pathetic creatures? Should I be ashamed of you?
What's my crime? I'm not bourgeois if I respect
the past – people have been fighting and dying
for rights since Adam. I'm not bourgeois if I enjoy
comfort – only if comfort defuses my angers against
injustice. I'm not bourgeois if I fear the evil in
men – that's human. If I enjoyed being *helpless* about
evil, you might call *that* bourgeois. If I indulged in
'Weltshcmerz', you might call *that* bourgeois. If I
pretended order existed when it didn't, you might
call that bourgeois. But if I try to create order out of
chaos, that's human. If I have loves and hates and
failures and regrets and nostalgias, if I'm weak and
frail and confused and I try to make order out of

the chaos of my miserable life, then that's human, bloody human, bloody bloody human!

ACT TWO PART FOUR – SECOND SPEECH

Table in a restaurant. MARY MORTIMER is dining with OLIVER MASSINGHAM, Under Secretary of State for Foreign Affairs. They are friends. She is slightly drunk.

MARY I've been told by my children that my only contribution to British journalism is to have elevated the gutter question 'who does he think he is?' to a respected art form… It *should* have hurt. Everything should hurt. But nothing does.

Oliver – this is off the record, but here's a question I've been dying to ask one of you only I didn't dare. It goes like this: you're a minister. I've watched the House in action: fights, battles of wit, of personality, intellect – but, that's not all is it? There's personality conflicts also – in the cabinet, in ministerial departments with cantankerous old civil servants. And then – tact! Diplomacy! Different kinds, in different ways, to different people. The public face on the one hand and the private reassurance to industry, the unions, the foreign ambassadors on the other. A great juggling act, wits alert all the time. And on top of this, on top – of all this, there's the problems of being a husband, a lover, a father, a friend, uncle, brother – God wot! (*Pause.*) How-do-you-do-it-for-God's-sake? How? How don't you become overwhelmed by it all? Do certain arteries harden? Is part of you callous? Like the doctor, or the writer? Tell me…

You think I'm very drunk don't you. But still functioning, eh? My lovely brain still ticking-tick-tick-tick-tick…

Me? Now that I'm drunk you want me to talk about myself for a change? Oh, well… I had a famous father, didn't you know? Famous for what they called in his day 'thought-provoking' novels. Only his thoughts provoked very few, very shallowly, and his day didn't last long. I used to taunt him in front of my university friends about having nothing to say to my generation and he used to take notice and rush to read my required reading. I had to grow up in his growing darkness and watch his lively pleasure, at being recognised in the streets, change into grey anonymity. He was a gentle man, made for the comforts fame brings and which the Gods gave him only a taste of. And I, with innocent devastation, went into competition with him. I won, of course. Because good fathers never let their children lose. He stepped back, graciously, for the sake of a healthy family, following the false principle, which many indifferent artists follow, that, if he couldn't create a healthy, happy family he couldn't create a worthy work of literature. He created nothing from that moment on. Defeated! And I understood none of that.

From *The Wedding Feast*

Synopsis:

Louis Litvanov is a shoe manufacturer with idealistic notions about the need to treat your employees as equals.

One evening his car develops a puncture, and while he waits for a wheel to be changed he finds himself outside a house from which come the sounds of a wedding.

He recognises the voices and realises it's the wedding of one of his employees.

Litvanov persuades himself that if he joins the wedding guests he will be warmly greeted, and admired for calling in to wish them well. He doesn't plan to stay but is persuaded to. Slowly he becomes drunk with them.

The proximity of their employer invites the abuse of his employees. The wedding party ends as a comic, chilling disaster.

PROLOGUE SCENE FOUR

LOUIS   Hammond is right. I talk and talk and only test my notions in the factory, but not in their houses. Here, for example, is one of my workers, Knocker White, just returned from a moving ceremony, full of hope, excitement, looking forward to his wedding feast. One of the most blissful days of his life, sharing it with his nearest and dearest, thanking them, with a banquet. Modest – naturally; poor – but gay. Full of genuine gladness.

What, what if he knew that outside, at this very moment, I, his boss, someone *he* felt was his superior, was toying with thoughts of coming in? What would he say? What would he feel if suddenly I *did* walk in? (*Thinks.*) Ha! Dumb! He'd be dumb with embarrassment. Stands to reason! I'd be in his way, upset everything. (*Thinks.*) Or would I? With anybody else, perhaps. But with me? A man who's known poverty half his life? How I'd transform that

embarrassment into a sweet pleasure, a real human
moment. (*Pause.*) What would happen? I'd go in.
Silence. They're amazed. Anxious. Dancing stops.
They back away. Understandable. But, I go straight
to the groom. A smile. Simple words. Tell him about
the puncture, the voices going for crates of beer, the
sound of music I heard, the coincidence. 'I don't
suppose you'll turn me out' I say. Turn me out? Ha!
He'll be ecstatic! He'll take my coat, rush to get me
an armchair, trrrremble with delight. And one by
one I'll make the acquaintance of the guests, the
bride, compliment her, tell jokes – about coming
again in nine months' time to be godfather. I'll beg
them not to stand on ceremony…

But not for self-honour. I won't be looking for
special attention, laurels, flattery, servile humbleness.
No! My actions will evoke nobler feelings. Our
conversation will be modest, natural, men facing
men in a human situation. For only a half hour, just
to offer respects, or perhaps an hour, and one or
two or maybe three drinks. But no more! Before the
food comes I'll leave. 'Business' I'll say. And they'll
understand that.

Then I'll leave, with a joke about the wedding bed
which'll make them roar with laughter, and then I'll
kiss the bride, gently, on the forehead, and I know
how they'll all look at me because it's a beautiful
gesture, in the right proportion, at the correct
moment, everything correct, most important. For to
every action is a time and place and they see that
I know that. And then, in the factory, next week,
the efficient industrialist. Kindly but firm. Not the
place to remember weddings and kisses. Work! The
world must turn on. The men must be fed, houses
built, shoes cut out and sewn up. Two sides! They'll
see two sides of me and when they're old they'll tell
their children and I'll be spoken of with affection,
honoured, remembered.

From *Shylock*

Synopsis:

Set in the Jewish Ghetto of Venice, 1563.

Shylock is a successful loan-banker with a passion for collecting old books. For the last ten years he's enjoyed the friendship of a world-weary Venetian merchant, Antonio.

Antonio's long-forgotten godson, Bassanio, a fortune-hunter, seeks out Antonio to borrow money in order to buy the wherewithal to woo Portia, an heiress.

Bassanio's friends are Lorenzo, a religious fanatic with political ambitions, and Graziano, an aristocratic clown with no skills other than to work in Antonio's warehouse.

Shylock's daughter, Jessica, falls in love with the dazzling Lorenzo.

Portia has inherited ruins which she intends to rebuild. Her foolish philosophical father bequeathed her an absurd command that she choose her husband with the help of three caskets.

Antonio's ships are at sea, he has no cash flow to help his godson and must borrow from his friend, Shylock. Shylock has no hesitation in lending Antonio whatever he wants.

Antonio asks for a contract. Shylock is offended that a contract is called for between friends. He refuses. Antonio insists, pointing out that the laws of Venice state there can be no dealings with a Jew unless a contract exists. The Jews of Venice depend upon the city honouring its contract with them therefore Shylock should honour the laws of Venice and sign a contract with Antonio.

Shylock is angry but concedes, proposing a contract so absurd that it will mock the laws of Venice which, he declares, mock the laws of friendship. The contract is for a pound of Antonio's flesh.

Antonio's ships are lost at sea. The contract must be fulfilled, the pound of flesh forfeited.

Lorenzo uses the incident for political gain pretending he stands against usury rather than against the Jew.

Portia enters the court, argues that the contract is a nonsense, and saves Shylock's life. But she cannot save his fortunes. He must leave for Palestine.

Antonio loses a friend, Portia has to marry a man she despises, Jessica realises too late she's married a religious bigot.

ACT ONE SCENE ONE

> *Venice 1563. The Ghetto Nuovo. SHYLOCK's study strewn with books and manuscripts.*

SHYLOCK So many books… And all hidden for ten years. Do you know what that means for a collector? Ten years? Ha! The scheme of things! 'The Talmud and kindred Hebrew literature? Blasphemy!' they said, 'burn them!' And there they burned, on the Campo dei Fiori in Rome, the day of the burning of the books. Except mine, which I hid, all of them, even my secular works. When fervour strikes them you can't trust those 'warriors of God'. With anything of learning? Never! Their spites, you see, the books revealed to them their thin minds. And do you think it's over even now? Look!

> *Pushes out a secret section of his bookcase.*

The Sacred Books. The law has changed and so the others I can bring back, but still, to this day, the Talmud is forbidden. And I have them, the greatest of them, Bomberg's edition, each of them. Aren't they beautiful? I'm a hoarder of other men's genius. My vice. My passion. Nothing I treasure more, except my daughter. So – drink! It's a special day.

Look! A present to cheer you up. One of my most treasured manuscripts, a thirteenth-century book of precepts, author Isaac of Corbeil, with additamenta made by the students. I used to do it myself, study and scribble my thoughts in the margin. We all did it. We had keen minds, Antonio, very profound we thought ourselves, commenting on the meaning of life, the rights and wrongs of the laws, offering

our interpretations of the interpretations of the
great scholars who interpreted the meaning of
the meaning of the prophets. 'Did the prophecies
of Daniel refer to the historic events or to the
Messianic times, or neither? Is the soul immortal,
or not? Should one or should one not ride in a
gondola on the Sabbath?' Money-lending was never
a full-time occupation and the Ghetto rocked with
argument – ha! It thrills me! (*Pause.*) There! I *have*
tired you.

ACT ONE SCENE ONE

SHYLOCK's study.

ANTONIO Those books. Look at them. How they remind me
what I am, what I've done. Nothing! A merchant!
A purchaser of this to sell there. A buyer-up and
seller-off. And do you know, I hardly ever see my
trade. I have an office, a room of ledgers and a table,
and behind it I sit and wait till someone comes in
to ask have I wool from Spain, cloth from England,
cotton from Syria, wine from Crete. And I say yes,
I've a ship due in a week, or a month, and I make
a note, and someone goes to the dock, collects the
corn, delivers it to an address, and I see nothing. I
travel neither to England to check cloth, nor Syria
to check cotton, or Corfu to see that the olive oil is
cleanly corked, and I could steal time for myself in
such places. It never worried me, this absence of
curiosity for travel. Until I met you, old Jew…and
I became caught up in your – your passion, your
hoardings, your – your vices!… You've poisoned
me, old Shylock, with restlessness and discontent…
A lawyer, a doctor, a diplomat, a teacher – anything
but a merchant. There's no sweetness in my
dealings. After the thrill of the first exchange, after
the pride of paying a thousand ducats with one hand
and taking fifteen hundred with the other – no skill.

Just an office and some ledgers. It's such a joyless
thing, a bargain. I am so weary with trade.

ACT ONE SCENE THREE

SHYLOCK's study.

SHYLOCK   Save the world with my knowledge? When I can't
be certain of saving myself? What a thought! Not
even the poor sages with all their wisdom could
save themselves. And poor sages they all were.
Constantly invited to run educational establishments
here and there, and never certain whether they
were running into a massacre. From the massacre of
Rouen they fled into the massacre of London; from
the massacre of London into the massacre of York,
and from the massacre of York no one fled! (*Pause.*)
Travelling wasn't very safe in those days!

Am I religious? What a question. Are you *so* drunk?
Religious! It's the condition of being Jewish, like
pimples with adolescence, who can help it? Even
those of us who don't believe in God have dark
suspicions that he believes in us. Listen, I'll tell you
how it all happened. Ha! The scheme of things! It
thrills me! Thrills me!

Imagine this tribe of Semites in the desert. Pagan,
wild, but brilliant. A sceptical race, believing only
in themselves. Loving but assertive. Full of quarrels
and questions. Who could control them? Leader
after leader was thrown up but, in a tribe where
every father of his family was a leader, who could
hold them in check for long? Until one day a son
called Abraham was born, and he grew up knowing
his brethren very, very well indeed. 'I know how to
control this arrogant, anarchic herd of heathens,' he
said to himself. And he taught them about one God.
Unseen! Of the spirit! That appealed to them, the
Hebrews, they had a weakness for concepts of the
abstract. An unseen God! Ha! What an inspiration.

But that wasn't all. Abraham's real statesmanship,
his real stroke of genius was to tell this tribe of
exploding minds and vain souls: 'Behold! An unseen
God! God of the Universe! Of all men! and –' wait,
for here it comes, ' – and, of all men you are his
chosen ones!' Irresistible! In an instant they were
quiet. Subdued. 'Oh! Oh! Chosen? Really? Us? To
do what?' 'To bear witness to what is beautiful in
creation, and just. A service, not a privilege!' 'Oh
dear! Chosen to bear witness! What an honour! Ssh!
No so loud. Dignity! Abraham is speaking. Respect!
Listen to him. Order!' It worked! *They* had God and
Abraham had *them*. But – they were now cursed. For
from that day moved they into a nationhood that
had to be better than any other and, poor things, all
other nations found them unbearable to live with.
What can I do? I'm chosen. I *must* be religious.

ACT ONE SCENE SEVEN

> *ANTONIO's house where he has just entertained*
> *LORENZO, BASSANIO, GRAZIANO and SHYLOCK.*
>
> *They have been discussing the nature of power.*
> *SHYLOCK disagrees with them all. Power lies in*
> *knowledge, he thinks. To prove which he tells them a*
> *potted history of Venice.*

SHYLOCK   Cassiodorus! The last and lovely link between
Imperial Rome and Gothic Italy. A sweet and
intellectual man. A statesman! A scholar! And
for what is this man remembered most? His
administrations on behalf of monarchs? Never!
During his life he'd succeeded in preserving
through all the devastations of civil wars and foreign
invasions a great collection of Greek and Roman
manuscripts, and – here is development one.

> *SHYLOCK tells his story with mounting excitement and*
> *theatricality, using whatever is around him for props,*

moving furniture, food, perhaps even people, like men
on his chessboard of history.

At sixty he retires to Brutti taking with him his
library of classics which he makes certain are
scrupulously copied by the monks. *What* a work!
What a faith! But why? Why should he have
bothered? What makes one man so cherish the work
of others that he lovingly guards it, copies, preserves
it? And a Christian, too, preserving the works of
pagans! From monastery to monastery the monks
were busy, busy, scribbling, for centuries, until the
book trade creeps from the monasteries into the
universities. The scholars take over from the monks.
The pattern takes shape.

Development number two: the destruction of the
Roman Empire! Italy breaks into three pieces. The
north goes to the German Holy Roman Empire, the
centre becomes dominated by the Papacy, and the
French house of Anjou takes over the South. Look
how fortunes change, rearrange themselves... Yes,
yes! I know about causes and effects. But – you read
me wrong if you believe I read history carelessly. I'm
perfectly aware how causes work their effects – but
within their time. The line *I* stretch joins together
men and moments who could never possibly have
forecast one another's acts. Did old Cassiodorus
working a thousand years ago see how Italy's
development would shape a thousand years later?
Of course he didn't! Hear me out. It's thrilling,
thrilling – believe me.

The land in three pieces, then. But does everything
stand still? Impossible! Watch in the north how
the German Holy Roman Empire disintegrates; in
the centre how the families of Rome brawl among
themselves; in the south how the French house of
Anjou fights the Spanish house of Aragon. Nothing
stands still! And as the dust of war and madness
settles what, gentlemen, is revealed? What?

City States! The magnificent City States of Milan!
Genoa! Florence! Venice! And every one of them
is left to its own government. What can it do? How
does one govern? Industry and trade grows. Can't
help itself. What! The centre of the Mediterranean
basin and *not* trade? So, as you know, you Italians
invent partnership agreements, holding companies,
marine insurance, credit transfers, Double-entry
book-keeping! Progress! But what else happened?
Don't forget old Cassiodorus lurking away patiently
down there in the sixth century. More business
meant more complex agreements, which meant
more law, which complicated the business of
government, which meant men of greater education
were needed, which meant a *new* kind of education,
more practical, more – ah! worldly! And where,
where I ask you, could that worldly, new education
come from to produce that new law, that new
government? Tell me. (*Pause.*) Why, from books!
Where else? And where *were* the books? Old
Cassiodorus! In the monasteries! He'd preserved the
ancient manuscripts of Rome and Greece, hallelujah!
Praise be to wise old men! Aren't you enjoying it?
Admit it, doesn't it thrill you to watch it take shape!
Be generous. Let yourselves go, for here comes
development three.

The year 1450. Two beautiful births: a wily old
German from Mayence named Gutenberg gives
birth to an extraordinary invention called the
printing press. And, at the same time, a great
classical scholar named Aldus Manutius is born.
Here! In our very own city of Venice, at the age of
forty-five, less than a hundred years ago, the great
Manutius sets up his divine press and produces the
incredible Aldine Editions. Suddenly – everybody
can possess a book! And what books! The works
of – Plato, Homer, Pindar and Aristophanes,
Xenophon, Seneca, Plutarch and Sophocles,
Aristotle, Lysias, Euripides, Demosthenes,

Thucydides, Herodotus, and all printed from
manuscripts kept and preserved in monasteries as far
apart as Sweden and Constantinople which Italians
were now bringing back home.

Amazing! Knowledge, like underground springs,
fresh and constantly there, till one day – up!
Bubbling! For dying men to drink, for survivors from
dark and terrible times. It thrills me! When generals
imagine their vain glory is all, and demagogues
smile with sweet benevolence as they tighten their
screws of power – up! Up bubbles the little spring.
Bubble, bubble, bubble! A little, little lost spring,
full of blinding questions and succulent doubts. The
word! Unsuspected! Written! Printed! Indestructible!
Boom! It thrills me!

> *Bells ring.*

> *SHYLOCK defiantly places his yellow hat on his head,
> bows, and goes off chuckling and mumbling…*

Bubble! Bubble! Bubble, bubble, bubble! Bubble,
bubble, bubble! Bubble! Bubble! Bubble…

ACT TWO SCENE ONE

> *Belmont. BASSANIO is confronting the three caskets.*

BASSANIO   What an eccentric test of love. Whose mind
constructed this? 'By his choice shall you know him'?

> *His tone of 'reasoning' is dismissive, arrogant and
> cunning throughout.*

What shall you know of him? That if he chooses
gold he will be a man without a soul, with a purse
where his heart should be? But a man without a soul
may have cunning, surely? Or he may love gold
but be plagued with guilt for doing so. Now there's
a man who'd shy away from the shiny stuff. No, I
don't see the point of such a simple trick.

And silver? What's one supposed to think of
that, stuck between gold and lead? Oh, here's the

mediocre man? Here's the man plays safe with life
and neither dares much nor achieves? Or is silver
the test of the temperate man, the sober man?
Perhaps the *diplomat* is being looked for here! The
statesman! Judge? Not unworthy men! Yet I hardly
riot in those qualities. Still, if such a man is wanted
for that extraordinary lady, and that extraordinary
lady is what I want, then perhaps the statesman,
diplomat and judge in me had *better* blossom. Hm!
Not such a simple test after all.

Come on now, Bassanio, use your wits. You've
not survived this far without an arsenal of guile.
Think! What father, wanting his daughter to marry
a statesman, diplomat or judge would devise such
a scheme? More to the point – does Portia look the
kind of a daughter who'd have the kind of father
who would *want* her to marry a statesman, diplomat
or judge? (*Pause.*) I will go mad.

The wrong approach! These caskets are more a test
for a sort, a kind, a spirit. The question then is: what
kind, what sort, what spirit would such a woman's
father want for her? The father! Look to the father.
He's the key. Good! That's something. So. The father
descends from a ruling aristocracy whose blood by
the time it reached her father, had been watered
down to the blood of a philosopher. And now,
abundant though the estates' possibilities are, yet
they're in ruin. Very decorous ruin, but – ruin. What
metal would a ruined ruinous philosopher choose?

> *Long pause, smile, he's seen through the strategy, but
> at first cunningly misleads.*

There can only be one answer. Simple! The end
of philosophy is despair. He looked around him,
saw the constant battles being fought, the waste,
disintegration and decay, and he concluded: for my
daughter, none of that! Gold! The hard, determined,
merciless pursuit of gain, security and comfort. Gold!
With gold is beauty bought and art, obedience,

the power for good. Gold! For my daughter shall
be trapped a man of gold. The sun is golden, the
harvest too – energy and sustenance. These things
I will, for my only child, these things which I with
my engagement in philosophy neglected to provide.
Gold!

Pause.

And then he changed his mind! For who can change
the habits of a foolish lifetime?

To PORTIA.

Lead, my lady. Lead I choose. My brain has battled.
There's its choice.

ACT TWO SCENE THREE

*SHYLOCK's study. He has been reading a letter from
JESSICA who has eloped with LORENZO. His sister
RIVKA has come to warn him that his bond with
ANTONIO is soon to be forfeited. SHYLOCK has been
trying to make light of it.*

RIVKA Talk with me. About the meaning of your bond,
talk with me. I'm not a fool… Clauses, meanings,
meanings, clauses! If *you* won't read the meanings
like a man, then this old woman will. What you
wanted to mock now mocks you! That's what your
bond means… In time? What time? The clocks will
soon strike six and that will leave only one day.

Don't be rude to me, Shylock! You have a friend.
Good. A Gentile and gentle man. Good. You made
some peace for yourself. I was happy for you. Good.
But could you leave it like that, my wise man, always
throwing his voice, his ideas about, on this, on that,
here, there, to anyone, could you leave it well alone
like that? Oh Shylock, my young brother. It made
me ache to watch you, looking for moral problems
to sharpen your mind, for disputations – as if there
weren't enough troubles inside these peeling walls.

But you *can't* pretend you're educated, just as you
can't pretend you're not an alien or that this Ghetto
has no walls. Pretend, pretend, pretend! All your life!
Wanting to be what you're not. Imagining the world
as you want. And now, again, as always, against
all reason, this mad pretence that Antonio's ships
will come in safe. (*Pause.*) You've mocked the law.
And not everyone in the Ghetto will agree to the
bending of the law, will they? Having bent the law
for us, they'll say, how often will the Venetians bend
it for themselves, and then we'll live in even greater
uncertainties than before. They'll be divided, as you
are, my clever brother. Who to save – your poor
people or your poor friend?

Well, am I a fool or not? Are there to be jokes or
not? Have you a problem or not?

Talk about it tomorrow? Tomorrow! Tomorrow!
What tomorrow? The clocks will soon strike six and
it will *be* tomorrow.

Me you can get out of the way, your problem – not!

ACT TWO SCENE THREE

> *SHYLOCK and ANTONIO have faced the awful fact
> that SHYLOCK must take a pound of his friend's flesh,
> and will in turn die for it.*
>
> *ANTONIO wants him to explain to the court how the
> bond came about.*
>
> *SHYLOCK insists that his 'pride must have its silence'.
> ANTONIO warns him the court will mistake silence
> for contempt.*

SHYLOCK   Perhaps they will be right. I am sometimes horrified
by the passion of my contempt for men. Can I so
lack pity for their stupidities, compassion for their
frailties, excuses for their cruelties? The massacres
by kings, the deathly little spites of serfs, the
oppressive jealousies and hurts of scholars who had

more learning than humanity. Seeing what men have done, I know the pattern of what they *will* do, and I have such contempt, such contempt it bewilders me.

Surely, I say to myself, there is much to be loved and cherished. Surely. I force myself to remember. Sometimes I succeed and then, ha! I'm a good man to know, such a good man. Children warm to me in the streets. They don't cry out 'Shylock Old Jew' then. No, they skip at my side and hold my hand, and on those days I walk so upright, like a young man, and I feel myself respected and loved. And love I myself also. Why, you ask, if joy comes through praising men, why do we not praise them all the time? The balance, dear friend, the balance! Take those books, one by one, place on one side those which record men's terrible deeds, and on the other their magnificence. Deed for deed! Healing beside slaughter, building beside destruction, truth beside lie. (*Beat.*) My contempt, sometimes, knows no bounds. And it has destroyed me.

ACT TWO SCENE FIVE

The court of the DOGE.

LORENZO has argued that usury is a sin.

ANTONIO disputes this.

ANTONIO The people suffer from ignorance, Lorenzo, believe me. To deprive them of knowledge is the sin…

You say a man is happy with no knowledge or art? There is wisdom in the wind, you say? The seasons tell all there is to know of living and dying? I wonder. Is it really understanding we see in the shepherd's eye? Is the tiller told more than the thinker? I used to think so, sitting with sailors roughened by salt, listening to their intelligence. They perceive much, I'd say to myself. But as I sat a day here, a day there, through the years, their intelligence wearied me. It repeated itself, spent

itself upon the same complaints, but with no real
curiosity. How alive is a man with muscles but
no curiosity? You wonder why I bind my fate to
Shylock, what I see in him? Curiosity! *There* is a
driven man. Exhilarating! I thank the shepherd for
my clothes and the tiller for my food, good men.
Blessed. Let them be paid well and honoured. But
they *know*, I, we know: there is a *variousness* to be
had in life. Why else does the labourer send his sons
to school when he can? He knows what self-respect
knowledge commands. All men do, wanting for their
children what fate denied *them*, living without meat
and keeping warm with mere sticks to do it. I'd have
died before now if no man had kindled my soul with
his music or wasn't there with his bright thoughts
keeping me turning and taught about myself. Yes.
Even at such an hour, I remember these things.
Don't talk to me about the simple wisdom of people,
Lorenzo. Their simple wisdom is no more than the
ignorance we choose to keep them in.

ACT TWO SCENE FIVE

Court of the DOGE.

*The DOGE insists that the people of Venice must
have justice. ANTONIO angrily dismisses this as an
hypocritical expectation.*

ANTONIO   Justice? For the people of Venice? The people?
When political power rests quite firmly in the
hands of two hundred families? That, though he
talks of principle, is what Lorenzo is impatient for,
to share that power. He uses the people's name
for through their grievances he'll come to power.
One of their grievances is what he calls usury. The
usurer's a Jew, and the Jew the people's favourite
villain. Convenient! Easy! But usury *must* exist in
our city. We have many poor and our economy
can't turn without it. The Jew practises what he hates
because we have forbidden him rights to practise

other professions. *He* relieves *us* of the sin. Do we condemn the Jew for doing what our system has *required* him to do? Then if we do, let's swear, upon the cross, that among us we know of no Christian, no patrician, no duke, bishop or merchant who, in his secret chambers, does not lend at interest, for that is what usury is. Swear it! On the cross! No one, we know no one!

Who's silent now? (*Beat.*) You will inflame the people's grievances in order to achieve power, Lorenzo, but once there you'll sing such different songs I think.

ACT TWO SCENE FIVE

Court of the DOGE.

LORENZO has realised that the court is being drawn into an anti-Semitic stance, and attempts to soften this by arguing Shakespeare's defence of the Jew. 'Hath not a Jew eyes etc etc', which infuriates SHYLOCK.

SHYLOCK   No, no, NO! I will not have it. (*Outraged but controlled.*) I do not want apologies for my humanity. Plead for me no special pleas. I will not have my humanity mocked and apologised for. If I am unexceptionally like any man then I need no exceptional portraiture. I merit no special pleas, no special cautions, no special gratitudes. My humanity is my right, not your bestowed and gracious privilege…

Jew! Jew, Jew, Jew! I hear the name around and everywhere. Your wars go wrong, the Jew must be the cause of it; your economic systems crumble, there the Jew must be; your wives get sick of you – a Jew will be an easy target for your sour frustrations. Failed university, professional blunderings, self-loathing – the Jew, the Jew, the cause the Jew. And when will you cease? When, when, when will your hatreds dry up? There's nothing we can do is

right. Admit it! You will have us all ways won't you?
For our prophecies, our belief in universal morality,
our scholarship, our command of trade, even
our ability to survive. If we are silent we must be
scheming, if we talk we are insolent. When we come
we are strangers, when we go we are traitors. In
tolerating persecution we are despised, but were we
to take up arms we'd be the world's marauders, for
sure. Nothing will please you. Well, damn you then!
(*Drawing a knife.*) I *will* have my pound of flesh and
not feel obliged to explain my whys and wherefores.
Think what you will, you will think that in any case.
I'll say it is my bond. The law is the law. You need
no other reason, nor shall you get it – from me.

From *One More Ride On The Merry-Go-Round*

Synopsis:

Jason, a Cambridge professor of philosophy, separated from his wife, Nita, is enjoying life with his mistress, Monica, a young American university lecturer.

He's contemplating the future. Should he retire and see more of the world, experience more of the life about which he philosophises?

In the first act he's full of contempt for his wife whose image he projects as dowdy and uninteresting. In the second act we discover that she's far from this image. Nita is dazzling, energetic, and has a young lover. We realise that both had wished the other to be what each became, but only after they were separated!

A comic plot about sophisticated personalities involving a recalcitrant daughter and the appearance of an illegitimate son who's a magician.

ACT ONE SCENE ONE, PHASE FIVE A

> *JASON's study. He's talking to MONICA about his wife, NITA.*

JASON I placed my goodbye note in the kitchen and she placed hers in the study. On the same day. But in rebellion against the stations allotted us in life we decided not to enter either place. And so a month passed before we knew what we'd done to one another. At which she giggled and I became furious… Oh yes, defend her! You're right. She's defendable. Defendable and dependable. But mad! Quite mad! 'A week's wage for the Third World!' Every family in Europe to give up one week's wage for training expertise, education, machinery… Worthy but – hare-brained! Committees all over Europe, experts working out what the money could be spent on, debates in the press, on radio, TV. Not charity but self-help. And – and this is her genius – she's doing it in two stages, getting pledges first so that when people give up their one week's wage, which they can pay in instalments, they won't feel it's done in isolation. Not *one* pledge to be called upon unless there's a 55 per cent response. It must be a majority wish also! Brilliant? Eccentric but practical, you say? But you didn't have to sleep with her!

Yes, that sounds outrageously frivolous, doesn't it? Outlining a socially responsible project and then following it up with complaints about sexual inadequacy. Confronted by such a worthy woman, thoughts of fucking her seem sacrilegious, contemptible, decadent! And yet, the day she came to me and outlined her...her...megalomaniacal project was the day I knew we had to separate. And I was right. She didn't simply accept the suggestion, she leapt at it. Feeding the needy Third World was more important than physically feeding needy me! And so it should be! By any standards whatsoever she'd got her priorities right. But I had to flee.

Those nights, oh those nights when I'd go to bed angry, my teeth clenched. Everything she *was* made *me* feel unworthy. Everything *I* wanted *she* made me feel was ignoble. So, defend her, as long as you understand the difference between you. *She* numbed me, with *you* each sense is heightened. She was *dutiful*, you *demand*. She was *silent*, you *tell* me your pleasure. With her I only wanted to complain about my bumptious colleagues and illiterate students, with you I want to walk through the streets of Paris, dance in New York, ski in the Alps; attend opera in Milan, theatre in London, ballet in Moscow; go yachting in the Mediterranean, trekking across the Kalahari, shopping in Samarkand – slumming it across the world! (*Beat.*) To her I was predictable, you – I have energies to surprise. (*Beat.*) You're not impressed? (*Beat.*) No one's ever loved you like I do.

ACT TWO SCENE ONE – PHASE FOURTEEN

NITA has just collected her daughter, CHRIS, from the airport. She has returned from staying on a kibbutz in Israel. CHRIS is twenty-four, beautiful and morose.

NITA And there's nothing more draining than relentless melancholy. You have that air about you makes everyone else feel guilty for bothering to live. (*Pause.*) Despair is habit-forming. (*Pause.*)

What an offspring you gave me, Lordee. (*Listening.*) What's that? I've too much energy? Well, I'm not going to apologise to her for that, Lord. It's not even true. If anything I didn't have energy enough. All day administrating stupid, oafish, female-resisting male civil servants, and in the evenings – flopped out, with her father complaining about his bumptious colleagues and illiterate students. Alibis! She's got an endless fund of alibis, haven't you?

You see, I've got this young lover, Lord, and I couldn't tear myself away after one of the most extraordinary nights you ever did witness, which, Lord, I suppose you did, very embarrassing, but you must be used to it by now, so, I was late, couldn't make the airport in time, and the lady superior here, fresh from a nunnery I think though they told me she was going to the Holy Land – anyway, this head nun here thinks it's all vaguely disgusting. Mothers shouldn't make love, let alone allow it to make them late for meeting a daughter at the airport. Terrible, dark significance in all that, of course. And isn't she making me suffer! Making me suffer well and truly, aren't you?

At least tell me that your twelve months working on a Kibbutz was not wasted. (*Pause.*) Did you meet any nice Jewish boys? Tell me what it was like being a Gentile among all those Jews. Although with your capacity for reproach and guilt-making they probably mistook you for one of their own. (*Pause.*)

At least smile at my wit. (*Pause.*) You're *never* going to smile are you, or talk, or get married? Might risk giving birth to a daughter who'd have a mother like me, eh? What about if it was a son with a mother like *you*?

ACT TWO SCENE ONE – PHASE SEVENTEEN

NITA's flat. She's talking to her daughter, CHRIS, about JASON.

NITA   On the phone we don't have to look at one another. When we look at one another *I* feel guilty for wanting more than he could give, and *he* feels guilty for having been inadequate. We make an uncomfortable couple, even divorced. (*Beat.*) We've bought a plot in the cemetery – we'll be *buried* together.

You don't understand what could have been so awful in a marriage that's lasted twenty-five years, do you? It's never made sense to you because no one talks about these things.

Long pause. Gathering steam.

I wanted to scream all the time. Walk around and scream and not stop.

She delivers what's known as a long, primal scream.

Even doing it *now* makes me feel good, not doing it *then*, keeping it in *then* was like allowing the spirit to become slowly toxic. I wanted to be taken and – and – and – oh – yes, fucked! No, don't be embarrassed, you want to understand.

He was a good man, even competent, but there was no – no – no urgency, no passion! I'm not talking about intenseness but about – oh – a wild gaiety, that's what I craved, an abandoned relentless, intoxicated, wild gaiety. I wanted to be seduced, slowly wound up, to play games of exposure and innocence, to be ravished with his eyes, to be

tongued, pursued, challenged, overwhelmed. I
wanted everything to be possible and permissible,
because what could be done in bed might, only
might, then be done in life. For us it was done in
neither place. We'd lie side by side, in the dark,
make tiny signs to one another, crawl here, crawl
there, a little of this, a little of that, meagre gestures
of love-play, then do it – once – sigh, roll apart, and
sleep. For another two weeks!

And do you know how often it happens with Matt?
Twice a day! And I don't come once but I come
and I come and I come and I come and I come
and I come! Within the space of an hour. Whoever
believed it could happen? A fantasy. But it did,
to me. (*Pause.*) I was once at a party and a young
smart-arse came up to me and brazenly asked me to
share his bed. A little thing in mind and spirit. And
when I declined he leaned over and said with his
damp arrogance, 'Pity!' And he pointed his finger up
and continued, 'Because you see that ceiling? I could
have taken you straight through there!' He couldn't
have lifted me high enough to get a sheet beneath.
But with Matt? He lifted me through the ceiling
and among the stars like a female sputnik, and I
haven't been down since. Reconciliation? To *what*?
An academic phallus that could only rise after a two
hour reading of *Paradise Lost* by which time paradise
was lost.

From *Caritas*

Synopsis:

In the 14th century a young woman, Christine Carpenter, breaks off her engagement and asks the church to allow her to live the rest of her life in a cell attached to the church in the Norfolk village of Pulham St Mary, in order to live the life of an anchoress. Through such austere living she hopes to become pure enough to receive divine revelation.

After three years she realises that an anchoress's life is not her vocation. Divine revelation eludes her. She asks the church to release her from her vows. They cannot. To do so, they argue, would be to make a cuckold of Christ. Because of a youthful decision she is doomed to live out her life imprisoned in her cell. She goes mad.

A metaphor for decisions, rooted in dogma, fanaticism or self-delusion, which we make in our youth and which imprison us for life.

THREE 'SAINT' STORIES FROM MATILDE

FIRST SAINT STORY, ACT ONE SCENE FIVE

> *CHRISTINE in her cell.*
>
> *MATILDE is an old gossip who every so often comes to sit by CHRISTINE's window to keep her company.*

MATILDE   You crossed your mouth? Good! An' your eyes an' ears an' your breasts? Good! For as the advice goes – an anchoress must love her window as little as possible, especially a young'un. There's men in this village with lewd eyes an' soft tongues, an' there's boys with taunts, an' old women with useless prattlin'. Your mother bring your food? Good! Now here's a story about a Belgie saint called Yvetta, tell me by a smithy who heard it from a nun who heard it from a pilgrimage to Rome which is how I get all my stories. Being a collector of stories 'bout saints which you'll be one day if you work hard at it. Yes! Get them from all over. Pilgrims. Vagabonds. Ole cooks at the fairs who I growed up with but them's old an' widows now. Full o' stories.

So, Yvetta. Sweet and pretty thing she were, an' happy, but, poor gal, she had to marry. Howsomever, when her husband die she renounce the world an' go to serve in a leper colony where she so much wanted to be a leper herself that she eat and drink with them, look, an' even wash in their bath water! Blust! You shouldn't catch *me* doin' that! An' when she were enclosed she were visited by that many temptations that she had to hev a hair cloth on her an' an iron chain with two heavy tablets hangin' round her neck, an' added to them she give her poor ole limbs a lot o' floggin', she did! She didn't eat too much, neither. Baked flour an' powdered ashes three times a week! An' all her day and nights were spent in prayers, tears, genuflexions, an' strikin' of the breast, an' when she sleep that were on sharp pointed stones. An' she die exactly on the day she say she were goin' to die. Hands outstretched and eyes raised to heaven. Seventy she was. An' they say that even though it were the middle of winter wi' a great storm of wind an' hail an' snow, yet the birds gathered round her cell an' sang as if it were a summer day. An' her face was all a brilliant glow, they say.

SECOND SAINT STORY, ACT ONE SCENE EIGHT

MATILDE You crossed your mouth? Good! An' your eyes an' ears an' breasts? Good! Your mother brought your food? Good! Now here's a story.

Saint Veridiana. Born 200 years ago they tell me, place called Siena in Italy. This one fasted even as a child, an' wore a chain an' hairshirt. *Her* cell were ten feet long an' only three and a half wide. No furniture, narthin', just a ledge in the wall an' two snakes for company. She tell her bishop they were sent in answer to a prayer that she be allowed to

suffer similar to what St Anthony did, 'cos you know
he were tormented by devils in the form of wild
beasts. They say them snakes sometimes lashed her
insensible with their tails. They killed one just before
she died, the other never returned. In summer she
slept on the ground, an' in winter on a plank with a
piece of wood for a pillow, an' now she wore an iron
girdle an' a hairshirt. Only one meal a day she had,
sometimes bread an' water, sometimes boiled beans,
most times narthin' 'cos she give it away to the poor
what used to come beggin' every night. Course she
don't talk to no one but the poor and afflicted, you
know. An' she live like that for thirty-four years. Till
she were sixty. Then she die. She also knew exactly
when she were goin' to die 'cos she sent for her
confessor, an' closed her windows. An' at the very
moment she die all the church bells began ringin'
by their selves, look. An' when they pulled down
the wall there she was, dead on her knees, with her
psalter open at the Miserere.

Pause.

Is that another comin' to your window? (*Shouting.*)
Go off there! That ent the right time o'day to be
callin'. (*To CHRISTINE.*) My, they do come don't
they? All wonder an' excitement an' reverence.
Think 'cos you cut yourself off from life you can
explain life's mysteries. (*Shouting to CHILDREN.*)
Get away, I say! (*To CHRISTINE.*) Your solitary life
make folk uneasy. Your fastin' make them feel their
greed. Your gentle ways make folk reflect upon their
violence. The church may be your anchor, gal, but
ha! She needs you, that she do.

THIRD SAINT STORY, ACT ONE SCENE TWELVE

MATILDE You crossed your mouth? An' your eyes, an' your
ears, an' your breasts? Good! Now here's a story. My
favourite. You'll like this one.

Saint Christiana. Another Belgie, an' she weren't an
anchoress or narthin', she were just – well, holy! A
spirit! A real spirit who could climb trees an' church
towers an' was so thin an' light from livin' in the
wilderness that she could sit on the thinnest branches
of trees, look, and sing psalms! There were three
sisters, three on 'em, an' she were given the job o'
lookin' after the cows. But did she mind? Course
she didn't. She'd sit out there contemplatin', an'
contemplatin', an' contemplatin' so much that she
put herself into a trance. Yes, a trance! An' that were
so deep they all thought she was dead, so they took
her to church, to be buried. But halfway through
mass she got off her bier an' clamber up the walls,
to the roof, look! An' she don't come down till her
mass is finished an' the priest promise to absolve
her. An' when she *do* come down she tell 'em all
how when she were dead she was shown purgatory,
hell, an' then paradise, an' they give her the choice
o' remainin' in heaven or sufferin' on earth for the
conversion of sinners. She come back! Cor, that
congregation fled! 'Cept for her eldest sister who
was too terrified to move. Glorious life she led. In
an' out of the wilderness, livin' on herbs, prayin',
contemplatin', prophesyin', hevin' ecstasies. Like a
sparrow she was, very weird and wonderful.

ACT ONE SCENE TEN

Interior of the church.

MATTHEW, CHRISTINE's priest, at silent prayer.
CHRISTINE at her prayers.

CHRISTINE … We adore thee, O Christ, an' we bless thee,
because of thy holy cross thou hast redeemed
the world. We adore thy cross, O Lord. We
commemorate thy glorious passion. Have mercy on
us, thou who didst suffer for us. Hail, O holy cross,
worthy tree, whose precious wood bore the ransom
of the world. Hail, O –

Stops abruptly. Ecstasy enters her voice.

Oh! Oh! A showing!

She can hardly believe it.

A showing! A showing! I have a showing. There
before me. I see the world's shape. God shows me
the world's shape. I see its joins, I see its links, I see
what clasps and holds it together. There's the hole
and there's the dowel, there's the dovetail, mortise,
tenon. Oh! Oh! I hear the flower blossom, see the
harvest grow, I know the colour of the wind, the
dark in light. Oh! Oh! It joins and locks and fits
and rhymes. That be no echo this time, Lord, I see
the shape. There is no mystery for Christine now.
Oh, blessed Jesus Christ, I begged and prayed and
prayed. The cross! The tree! The precious wood!
And you have give to me a showing, you have give
to me a showing!...

The dark in the light? Did I say 'the dark in the
light'? I *did* say 'the dark in the light', didn't I?
(*Pause.*) That were no showing then. (*Beat.*) Though
it did make sense. Gone. An' I nearly named the
parts. (*Pause.*) There's a foul stench in my cell. Arrgh!
Who'll rid my cell of its foul stench?

Long pause.

(*To MATTHEW, hissing.*) Go away!

TWO SPEECHES FROM THE TRAVELLING PRIEST, ACT ONE SCENE THIRTEEN

*Inside the church. A TRAVELLING PRIEST is giving
a 'sermon' to a congregation.*

TRAVELLING
PRIEST 'Blow ye the trumpet in Zion, and sound an alarm
on my holy mountain.' Thus saith the prophet
Joel. New sermons are being preached in our land,
beloved. Here's one for you: to each man hath
God given conscience. Dominion over himself!

Therefore turn to your priests and tell them this: one vicar cannot be upon the earth, for each is vicar to himself.

'Beat your ploughshares into swords, and your pruning hooks into spears: let the weak say I am strong.' Thus saith the prophet Joel. One hundred thousand men are gathered under Wat Tyler, brothers. Canterbury opens her gates, the manor records burn and they have snatched the mad John Ball from jail to sing his lovely sermons to us all. Have you ever heard John sing, beloved?

'Good people' sings John Ball, 'good people, things will never go well in England as long as goods be not in common held. By what right' sings he, 'are they who are called lords greater folk than we? Clothed in velvet, warm in furs and ermines, while we are covered with rags! Tell me' sings John Ball, 'when Adam delved and Eve span, who was *then* the gentleman?' D'you like those songs, brothers and sisters? They sing them from the coast of Kent up to the Wash.

'And it shall come to pass afterwards that I will pour out my spirit on all your flesh; and your sons and your daughters shall prophesy, your old men shall dream dreams, your young men shall see visions.' Thus saith the prophet Joel… 'Help truth and truth shall help you!'…

> 'Now reigneth pride in price
> And covertise is counted wise
> And lechery withouten shame
> And gluttony withouten blame…
> (*Fleeing.*) 'God do bote,* for now is tyme!

*God do bote – God claims

ACT ONE SCENE FIFTEEN

Carpenter's workshop. TRAVELLING PRIEST lays the dead ROBERT, CHRISTINE's ex-fiancé, gently into wood shavings. others are around.

TRAVELLING
PRIEST London, the Friday after the feast of Corpus Christi, the boy King meets Wat Tyler at Mile End, agrees to his demands. I watch it happen. Watch the King bow to his people, listen to the roar, the cheer go up. Shivers down my spine. Exhilarating.

Then the mood changes. People become intoxicated with their games and powers. A people's court behead Sudbury and Hales, and at the Tower the King's physician, which intoxicates their passions more. Then the crude and rough ones surface. Scum arising to the top to pay off ancient scores and murder aliens.

I shout and warn but there are quick and easy tongues to call me traitor. Oh, those quick and easy tongues! We come to Smithfield where we give the King a second paper of demands. 'Come talk to us' he says. Again I warn but oh the tongues were quick and easy. Wat the Tyler goaded by the quick and easy mob steps to the other side where – swish! The Mayor of London kills him quick and easy. That was that!

The freedom charters are withdrawn. John Ball sings his last sermon and is hung, drawn and quartered at St Albans, and the rest come home. (*Looking at the dead ROBERT.*) One way or another.

ACT TWO PARTS NINE,TEN,ELEVEN

> *CHRISTINE in the corner of her cell. She cradles the heavy crucifix in her arms. Laments and rocks backwards and forwards.*

CHRISTINE   The poor wail, the orphan sighs, the widow is desolate, the pilgrim needs water, there's danger for the voyager, hardship for the soldier, cares for the bishop. Come to me, come to me, come, come, come, come. (*Pause.*) I've loved him from cradle time. No smile like my baby's. See, they humiliate him now. *I* can't comfort him, though. I've loved him from his first falls. No cry like my baby's. See, there are thorns on his head. *I* can't comfort him, though. Was anythin' so tender? The smell of oil on his skin, the trust in his eyes as I wrapped him warm. See, they've given his poor body a cross to bear. Why don't *my* bones crack instead? I can't comfort him though. And that first word he spoke. Such cleverness. How swift he learnt. See, they nail him now. My lovely boy, my own, my flesh, my blood. And did I feed an' watch you grow an' guard you 'gainst the plagues for this? An' did we look at blue skies, the matin' mare, the suckin' lamb, the settin' sun, an' watch the rivers runnin' – for this? (*Cries out.*) Put nails through me! Through my hands, my feet. Me! Me! Oh, the ache, the ache, the helpless ache. I can't bear it! Can't bear it! Cannot. Oh, oh…

The poor wail, the orphan sighs, the widow is desolate, the pilgrim needs water, there's danger for the voyager, hardship for the soldier, cares for the bishop. Come to me, come to me, come, come, come, come, come…

> *CHRISTINE squeezes one bare breast, part caress, part maternal longing, intoning:*

The poor wail, the orphan sighs, the widow is desolate, the pilgrim needs water, there's danger for the voyager, hardship for the soldier, cares for the bishop. Come to me, come to me, come, come, come, come, come, come, come...

Long pause. A new mood fills her. She leaps up, backs against the wall, addresses MATTHEW in her mind.

It's my thoughts, father, I can't put my thoughts on *him*. I see him on the cross, I see that sweet face sufferin', I see that poor body hangin' limp on its nails, an' I feel the pain here an' here an' here an' here an' here, an' I stand with my back to the wall, my arms outstretched (*Movements follow words.*) my eyes closed, an' I cry out, 'Lord Jesus, sweet Lord, I'm with you, here I stand, I feel the pain, I'm with you.' An' then, an' then – oh forgive me, father, forgive me! – but as I stand, my arms outstretched, my eyes closed – I think new thoughts which I can't deny. (*Her legs move apart.*) 'cos, oh, they're sweet, so sweet. I'm naked. My body open to the sky, my skin in the grass, sun on my breasts. I feel cool winds bring me the smell of hawthorn an' the wild mint. An' I see the birds sweep high an' singin'. An', oh, those clouds, those glorious rollin' shapes, that sweet scent, that soft air – thaas not the devil's forms, I say. Forgive me, father, but I say thaas never the devil's forms. An' I'm torn between shame an' delirium. The spring, Father, the spring! I am crucified upon the spring!

She screams. Desolate. Then –

What next?

She looks around her cell, turns to a wall, places her hand on it, mumbles to herself, turning her head slowly around her 'prison'.

This is a wall, and this is a wall, and this is a wall, and this is a wall, and this is a wall, and this is...

From *When God Wanted A Son*

Synopsis:

Joshua, professor of semantics, is Jewish; Martha is Gentile. They were married and are now separated.

Connie is their daughter struggling to be a comedienne. Her humour is sophisticated and sardonic. She's not having much success.

She returns home for comfort and to attempt to reconcile a confused background.

Her mother, attempting to dabble in the stock market, is a closet anti-Semite.

Joshua returns to attempt to persuade her to forget and forgive and to invest money in his project to build a machine that will detect true character through the inflections of the human voice.

Martha tries but can't bring herself to accept him. He's too uncomfortable a personality.

The play argues that anti-Semitism, like stupidity, is here to stay.

TWO CABARET APPEARANCES BY CONNIE

ACT ONE SCENE ONE

> *A rough cabaret club.*
>
> *CONNIE stands before her audience fearing the worst. Her material seems to amuse only her. Prominently hanging around her neck is a gold chain from which hangs a Star of David. Her 'audience' is not us but a gathering slightly off stage.*

CONNIE   Poland, 1875. Moshe Ben Levy. The richest Jew in his village. Comes the Cossack pogroms, Moshe's store – no chance. Burned to the ground. Stock looted, son murdered, daughter abducted, wife dead from a broken heart. Poor Moshe Ben Levy. Down to his last crust of bread, his last pat of butter, the last leaves of tea, the sugar gone. You couldn't get lower than Moshe was in that year of 1875, in the heart of Poland, in the heart of winter, heartbroken and cold. Surely this was the end.

He places the last of his logs on the fire, fills the kettle for the last leaves of tea, toasts his last crust of bread, butters it with the last pat of butter. Then, as though God hasn't punished him enough for sins he can't even remember committing – the last of his calamities.

The water boils. He reaches for kettle. He's shivering from the cold. He's clumsy. Brushes against the last piece of toast buttered with the last pat of butter – plop! To the floor! The filthy floor!

Now, everyone knows that toast falls butter side down. Always! Without fail. But not this day. This day – a miracle. Moshe's toast, which should have fallen butter side down, falls butter side up! Is this an omen? A sign that his luck is about to change? He rushes off to the Rabbi.

'Rabbi, Rabbi. You know me, Moshe Ben Levy, once rich now poor, my son murdered, my daughter abducted, my wife dead from a broken heart. But, Rabbi, this morning, this morning I knocked my toast to the floor and it landed butter side up! A miracle! Everyone knows that toast lands butter side down, always, without fail, tell me, is it an omen? Is my luck about to change?'

The Rabbi thinks and thinks and says: 'I have not wisdom enough to interpret this sign alone. I must confer with the other Rabbis. Return tomorrow morning. You will have our answer.'

Moshe falls asleep only for one hour before the sun rises. All night his imagination is on fire with visions of a new life. Without washing or changing his shirt, pausing only to gabble his morning prayers, Moshe Ben Levy hurries to the Rabbi's house. The Rabbi emerges tired from a room full of tired Rabbis, grey and numb with the meaning of life.

'Rabbi, Rabbi' cries the eager, demented Moshe. 'Tell me, the miracle, what does it mean? My toast that landed butter side up – is it an omen? Is my luck about to change?'

His language is Yiddish, of course.

The Rabbi replies. Also in Yiddish, of course. 'We have stayed awake all night. Seven of us. The wisest in the district. We have prayed, we have argued, we have referred to the Holy books. One of us even dipped into the Cabbala to search for the meaning of your toast, which landed butter side up. And we have concluded (*Despair and sadness.*) you must have buttered your toast on the wrong side.'

> *CONNIE cups her mouth and yells as though she were one of the audience.*

Gerroff! Women shouldn't tell jokes! You've *never* told a good joke and you never *will* tell a good joke!

> *Becoming herself, she smiles ingratiatingly.*

Thank you, thank you, I thought you'd like that one.

> *Her smile of gratitude turns into contempt.*

CONNIE'S SECOND APPEARANCE, ACT ONE SCENE THREE

CONNIE All right! All right! So I'm not funny. I'm funny but I'm not *very* funny. You don't like my jokes so let's play a game instead. Let's divide the world.

I believe the world's divided into those who are clever and are massacred, and those who are stupid and do the massacring. (*Pause.*) Come on now, you tell me how *you* think the world is divided. (*Beat.*) I believe the world's divided into those who are clever and are massacred, and those who are stupid and do the massacring. How do *you* think it's divided?

Silence.

You want another example? Right. Here's another example. I believe the world's divided into those who applaud achievement and those who begrudge it – pah pom!

Silence.

Thank you, thank you. I thought you'd like that one.

ACT ONE SCENE THIRTEEN

CONNIE's room, full of notes on the wall, left by her father. She holds toy phone.

CONNIE   You should have trusted me, Billy Boy. There was evidence enough. I'd hit days of chaos, that's all. Couldn't you tell? Every gal hits her days of chaos. Most have it every three years. The menstrual cycle of despair.

Let me tell you about the ages of women. Age the first: little girl. Little girl in awe of loud-mouthed male intimidation. Sometimes little girl in competition with loud-mouthed male intimidation. Sometimes little girl turns intimidator and leads squad of mocking girls to diminish male pride.

Age the second: breasts! Little girl with big breasts. A new confidence or a new intimidation? Should she be afraid to be stared at or should she use them to command attention? I used them to command attention. Breasts turned me into a woman. Nothing turned boy into man. I was ahead.

But not for long. Age the third: young woman! and – pah pom! Male expectations! Which were either crude or unfathomable. He groped you or demanded you appear in a certain way. From which followed – chaos. And so the menstrual cycle of despair began, Billy Boy. One day I was busy trying to be what I thought you wanted me to be. Next day

I was as unfeminine as possible. If he wants me he'll
have to take me for *who* I am not what I *look* like.

Stupid woman! I hadn't understood that what I
look like reveals who I am. As everything does. The
way I walk, talk, gesticulate, think about the world.
Stupid woman! Stupid theories! I bristled with
them. You must have felt you were making love to a
porcupine, Billy Boy. Bit of a pain in the arse, was I?

Here, I have a Norfolk joke for you. An old, old
widow called on her Parson with a problem. 'Parson'
she say, 'Parson, I see my dead husband today, sittin'
in his old chair next to the fire. What do it mean
d'yer think?' 'Could mean many things' say the
Parson. 'What do *you* think it means?' 'Well' say the
old dear, 'they do say it could mean rain.'

Oh, Billy Boy, you should have persevered. I'm not
arrogant. It's just that half of me is my father's child.

> *She puts down phone. Drifts to another note on the
> wall. Reads:*

'If you think education is expensive you should try
ignorance!'

ACT ONE SCENE FIFTEEN

> *CONNIE's room. CONNIE and MARTHA, her
> mother.*

MARTHA Most women are married to men who bore them.
Have you noticed that? They sit around in pubs,
restaurants, social gatherings, with faces announcing
to the world that they deserve more from life.

Men confuse that bored look with female mystery.
It challenges them. Up they trot. 'I understand' they
say. But they don't. Within five minutes of their
conversation it's painfully obvious they don't. They
bore.

But 'he' understood. 'Women have the power to
give or deny happiness' he once said, 'and through

that power we are manipulated.' He hated being at anybody's mercy.

I couldn't bear him.

And he was full of opinions. He *knew* who was a great writer, a great painter, a great composer. He could actually say Bach was boring. Passionately say it. It mattered to him. Me – I was exhilarated by them all, Bach, Mozart, Mahler. Well, perhaps not Mahler so much. Too solemn. Still, that's just *my* taste. When you're *that* great, dismissive opinion seems irrelevant. Presumptuous! Absurd! But he insisted: opinions made you a person. 'It's a guarantee of your freedom,' he'd yell at me. Always impatient. Him and his circle.

Frightening lot they were. Non-stop talkers. Opinions on this, opinions on that. How can people have so many opinions about the world? You'd think it was such a vast and complex place they'd be confused most of the time. Not that lot. Solutions for and opinions about everything and anything.

Not me. Nothing much changes about human beings I always think. And the world we live in seems to be shaped by scientists and inventors not by people with opinions. You take the opinion that everyone should work. Work dignifies people! The work ethic! Along comes the silicon chip and suddenly we have – the leisure ethic! Opinion changes! Everyone's demanding more leisure for all.

What *was* it about him that I hated? What really was it? Even now as I think about him my teeth clench. He had an air. He had – an air.

ACT ONE SCENE TWENTY ONE

CONNIE's room.

JOSHUA has unexpectedly returned asking that 'we turn our swords into ploughshares. For remember: when God wanted a son he crawled up the skirts of a Jewish girl!'

His unannounced appearance and his declamation send MARTHA into an hysterical outburst which begins, continues and ends on the same high, intense level as though she has become possessed.

MARTHA (*Screaming.*) Ahhhh! No! Tell him to go! Do you hear how he comes with offence? Look at him. He walks into everyone's room that way, as though he were born there, as though he can say anything anywhere anytime. We agreed. You promised. My home, my decisions, my privacy. Not everybody wants you around. Not everybody thinks God chose you to be their neighbour. Tell him to go. Tell him I can't bear anything about him – his arrogance, his opinions, his irreverence. No reverence for anything, only what *he* thinks, what *he* wants, what *he* believes. Him! Him! Him!

Don't laugh at me. Do you hear his laughter? Do you hear his superior laughter? So superior, so confident, so happy, so eager, so interested, so talkative, so fucking full of his own fucking self. Listen to me. He makes me curse. He's made me decadent. He's never respected me. Destroyer of innocence, lecher, devil! Tell him to go. Tell him the world wasn't made for him. Tell him people want to be left alone. He disturbs everyone. Everyone feels unsafe, threatened. Look at him looking at me. His eyes mocking me. He always mocked me. Some of us have our own beliefs, some of us don't care what you believe. We care about our *own* little thoughts. Yes! Little to you, precious to us. Look at him! Full of contempt and derision. One day someone will

gouge his cockiness from his eyes. Tell him that. Tell
him to go. Before it's too late. Tell him he's an old
man who's been in the world too long. Tell him he
doesn't belong in this house. Tell him I can't breathe
when he's in the room. I never know what I feel
when he's in the room. I don't know what to do
with my hands, where to look, what to say. Listen to
me, my words are all jumbled. I'm screaming. He
makes me scream. As soon as I see him I go into
shock, I become unnatural, I hate myself. Tell him to
go. Tell him to go. Tell him to go go go. I can't stop
screaming. Tell him to go.

ACT TWO SCENE SEVEN

JOSHUA is talking to his daughter, CONNIE.

JOSHUA   There was the time you tried to milk a bull... We
used to go on holiday each year, for about four
years running, to a little farm sublet by one of
your mother's brothers from his two thousand
acre estate – for a not inconsiderable rent, I might
add. You were ten years old and you'd seen the
farmer's wife sitting on a stool with a pail between
her legs pulling at something hanging, so *you* got
a stool and put a pail between your legs and you
found something hanging and you pulled! What
happened? He kicked! You pull a bull's ding-dong he
gets confused. He say 'Who dat dere? Who dat dere
pulling my ding-dong when I ain't ready to have my
ding-dong pulled. Dat my ding-dong. *I* tell you when
I ready to have my ding-dong pulled.' (*Laughter.*)
Fortunately the pail was in the way.

(*Quieter now.*) I remember we took you to concerts
and theatre and on long journeys to foreign parts.
You liked puddles, I remember.

   Pause.

'The first truth' says Buddha, 'is that all life is
suffering.'

Sad smiles.

Do we really accept that? Really, really accept that?

The question hangs in the air.

What do you mean you're sorry you were none of
the things I wanted you to be? *Wanted* you to be?
Wanted? Only one thing I *wanted* you to be – was
free. Independent. Dependent upon no one. Not
a husband for your keep, not a country for your
identity, not a group for your cause, nor an ideology
for your fulfilment. I wanted you to learn your way
out of prisons. To be nobody's slave, nobody's guest.
You make people laugh. I'm not complaining… I
can even teach you one or two things about laughter.

You want to know about laughter? Let me tell you
about laughter. Laughter comes from the Jews. Why
the Jews? Because we're a nervous people. When
you invent God you make people uneasy. When
you then say he's chosen you to bear witness to the
beauty of his creation and to guard his justice you
make people feel indignant. 'We have our own Gods,
we have our own justice.' But does the Jew listen?
He can't! When you've invented God no other
authority can really be taken seriously. And so the
Jew questions all authority. People don't like that.
They burn you for it. Isn't that enough to make you
nervous? Nervous people laugh. And that doesn't
help either.

(*Looking up.*) You there? I'm talking to you. We've
got problems down here. You sure you put the parts
together in the right order?

(*To CONNIE.*) He even questions the authority he
claimed was unquestionable. What can you do with
such a people? And they write funny books about it
all.

Look at the Bible, the largest collection of jokes
in the world. The Book of Job. What could be
funnier? To prove Satan wrong God lets him

play dice with Job's fortunes. A man who had
everything – beautiful wife, lovely children, wealth,
a house in the country on the west bank, and then,
all of a sudden, wham! He loses everything. His wife
dies, his children all die, his car, his hi fi, his washing
machine – everything repossessed! *And* he's struck
down with herpes. It's enough to make you nervous.
So what does Job do? If he were a Christian, faith
would be enough. But for a Jew nothing is enough.
He has to go to the top.

(*Looking up.*) You there? I'm talking to you. I've got
problems down here. I'm an upright man, I take a
little here give a little there. Is this just? Look at me.
I'm a mess.

And what does God do? He laughs back. He shows
Job a big fish, a leviathan he calls it. 'Can you hook
it?' God asks. 'It's a big fish' says Job. 'How can
I hook it?' 'Right!' says God. 'How much more
difficult to hook me!' 'He's doing a Hamlet on me'
says Job. 'Very funny!' And he's right – what could
be funnier?

The Jew can't help it, he questions authority with
laughter. It's a nervous tic.

Take Einstein. Einstein questioned authority with
laughter. You know how it is. You meet a Jew on the
stairs and you ask him if he's going up or he's going
down and he says, 'Well, it depends. Everything's
relative!'

Take Freud. Freud questioned authority with
laughter. 'Ernest,' he said to his biographer,
Ernest Jones – another Jewish habit, talking to
your biographer – 'Ernest, I'm half convinced
by socialism.' 'How come, Herr Doktor?' Ernest
knows the Herr Doktor is a thorough conservative.
'Well,' says Freud, 'I've been reading Trotsky on
socialism' – Trotsky, another funny man who
questioned authority – 'I've been reading Trotsky
and he says that in the first phase of the transition

to socialism there will be big problems: upheavals, misery, large-scale disaster. But in the second phase – the promised land for us all, paradise on earth, utopia! Well, Ernest, I am convinced about the first half.'

No, don't laugh. This Jewish humour, this laughing at authority, it causes such irritation. You're not supposed to laugh at the misery they bestow on you. It's unnatural. It causes a great deal of misunderstanding, better known as anti-Semitism, or anti-Zionism as the new jargon will have it. And what *is* anti-Semitism? It's hating Jews more than is necessary. It's enough to make you nervous. Especially when you're never certain whether you've got an audience out there or a lynch mob.

From *Lady Othello*

Synopsis:

Stanton, professor of American literature, married with two children, has – in the course of a lecture tour – fallen in love with Rosie, a black, New York 'mature' student.

He's returning to New York to spend time with her and discover the true depth of his feelings.

The play charts their riotous, sad, comic, bawdy days together during which he realises it can't work.

ACT ONE SCENE FOUR

> *Airport coach into New York.*
>
> *ROSIE, stunning, radiant, off-beat, a beautiful Jamaican-black New Yorker. She's talking to STANTON.*
>
> *ROSIE chatters at a ferocious rate, which she does well, fluently and frequently.*

ROSIE And then Stella-Bella, my flatmate, rings up from downstairs by the porter's desk and says, 'Rosie, it's here, didn't you see it?' And I say, 'What's here?' 'Your results, dumb-dumb,' she says. 'An envelope, here, with a university's name on it.' 'Stella-Bella', I say, 'you've forgotten what time it is. I haven't even brushed my teeth yet' – because sometimes as a waitress she's on early shifts for breakfasts and gets back around ten, ten-thirty, and maybe I've had a late night 'cos sometimes I do late shifts in the same restaurant to subsidise the lousy alimony cheque I get from my cautious, anxious, mean-as-arsehole ex-husband, and I say to her, 'Stella-Bella', I say, 'now you come straight up with that envelope because I'm in no fit state to leave this flat and I don't care how late you are this is life or death for me.' And she was kinda eager herself to know, was

I going to be allowed entry into the hallowed halls
and groves of academe for a second chance in life or
not, so she rushes up shrieking, 'I'm late! I'm late!'
and I tell her, 'Stella-Bella, pray! I'm opening the
envelope, pray!' Which she did. Stood there like
a madonna – a Jewish madonna, you understand,
because with a name like Stella-Bella she couldn't
come from Neapolitan Catholic stock, you know
what I mean? And she prayed. In Hebrew!
'Stella-Bella', I said, 'do you know what you're
saying because I don't want you mumbling the
incomprehensible to the Almighty…'

Yes, they accepted me!

ACT ONE SCENE FIVE

> *ROSIE's apartment. She's on the phone to a friend.*

ROSIE   (*Whispering.*) Oh hi, Merle. Yes. He's here. What
d'you mean, how do I feel? I feel like a lump
of jelly, that's how I feel. I feel like I'm back at
college with a crush on my lecturer, which is what's
happened of course, only now I'm a mother! No,
we haven't talked yet. What chance have we had?
This guy flew in a couple of hours ago, did my son's
homework with him then zonked out. And I'll tell
you something else, Buster, I'm not letting him talk
tonight either. This lascivious woman has other plans
for the English gentleman's native tongue. Mark's
with his friend, Stella-Bella's got Chinese take-away
and a Gary Cooper movie, and that leaves me the
professor and a free lounge and I tell you neither
his views on modern American literature nor my
views on everything are gonna be taking the floor
tonight because I tell you – he is more beautiful than
I remembered and I'm more in love than I knew
was possible so if you want news about how my
future looks you'd better hang up now and don't call
us we'll call you. Do I make myself plain or do you

want me to repeat all that? (*Long listening pause.*) Oh,
Merle, that's awful. I didn't know your father had
gone into hospital. Yeah – sure sixty is young these
days. Keep me in touch. Byeee!

ACT ONE SCENE ELEVEN

ROSIE's apartment.

*STANTON has just asked her what her PhD thesis
will be.*

ROSIE Passion! Men are driven by passions. Makes
them irrational. The conduct of political affairs
is perverted by irrational men. That'll be my
thesis. Surprises you, huh? Coming from a woman
who's driven by passions which make her behave
irrationally?

You take protest. Nothing wrong with protest. Sign
of a healthy society. What goes wrong? I'll tell you
what goes wrong. People! They fuck it up. Start off
wanting more democratic rights, end up wanting to
overthrow democratic institutions. People!

You take commerce. People rage against capitalism.
Nothing wrong with trading. Healthy instinct. What
goes wrong? I'll tell you what goes wrong. People!
They fuck it up. Get greedy. Produce cheap goods.
Form totalitarian monopolies which become a law
unto themselves. People!

You take politics. Nothing wrong with politics. It's
the art of government. We have to be governed.
Since Adam! So what goes wrong? I'll tell you what
goes wrong. People! They become politicians, fuck
up politics. Ambitious! Dishonest! Opportunist!
People!

You take religion. Nothing wrong with wanting
to believe in a God. Jesus! Buddha! Mohammed!
They're all saying the same thing – be good, love
one another, look after the kids! So what goes

wrong? I'll tell you what goes wrong. People! They become fanatics. Scream at one another. 'I'm holier than thou and all must be as holy as me!' People!

You take science. 'Science will blow up the world! Pollute the earth!' Bullshit! You wanna attack Newton, Galileo, Benjamin Franklin? Science gave me my contact lenses and saved Mark dying from diphtheria. So what goes wrong? I'll tell you what goes wrong. People! Along come the crooked industrialists, the dishonest politicians and the righteous fanatics, and *they* fuck up science. People!

She's finished and beams her full power upon STANTON who is sagging.

Guess I tired you out, huh? And we haven't even started tonight's studies, honey.

ACT TWO SCENE TWO

FRANCESCA's restaurant, ROSIE's and STANTON's favorite. FRANCESCA talks to them.

FRANCESCA   Lovers, lovers, lovers! I love lovers… Some people hate them, you know. Nothing drives them madder than to see two people kissing. Love's an affront. You ever thought about that? Love's an emotion so charged and pure that it can attract a pure and charged hatred. That's why I don't think lovers should love in public. Some people have murder in their eyes when they see lovers and somewhere out there is a person so disappointed with their life, so full of self-contempt, they're carrying murder in their pocket. A gun to blow away lips that were blowing kisses. (*Imitates a gun.*) Pyeach! Pyeach! 'Put that tongue back in your mouth, lover!' Pyeach! Pyeach! 'Put them arms down by your sides, lover!' Pyeach! Pyeach! 'Wipe that shine from your eyes, lover! Who gave you the right to be happy when I'm not?' Pyeach! Pyeach! So drink up, lovers. Here you can hold hands, gaze at each other, touch and blow kisses. You're safe. Drink!

From *Bluey*

Synopsis:

Hilary Hawkins is a judge who's reached a crisis of confidence. An incident from the past, which he has suppressed, has been working corrosively within his subconscious.

A particularly nasty court case stirs his memory. Through a series of events, and in the course of writing his diary, he remembers the incident: in his student days he had worked on a building site, reluctantly became involved in stealing lead from a roof that a group of them were repairing. His task was to throw the lead down and shout a warning each time before doing so. On one occasion he forgets to shout, and is accidentally responsible for scarring the plumber, Ron's, face.

At the height of his crisis he goes in quest of the plumber. When he finds him he can only stand and observe him from a distance imagining three possible outcomes of a confrontation he has not the courage to face.

PART ONE

> *JUDGE HILARY HAWKINS is continuing his diary about an old sweetheart from his youth.*

HILARY I did not ring. I made no contact at all. She had been so pretty, such a sweet and generous soul, I just could not face her dying. That bloated skin hairy from the drugs, I would have wept and she would have seen her dying in my eyes. I was not strong enough for the pain of that. Something had snapped and I was beginning to turn away from disaster stories in the press, to weep at the sight of starving children on television, rage if I saw rudeness or insensitivity in my children. No matter how ashamed I was to be incapable of that comfort some have and can hand to others – there it was! I could not go.

Audrey would have come to *my* deathbed. With all her lack of sophistication, her absence of what is called 'good taste' *she* would have found the right tone of voice, pitched her sunniness at the right angle, not too high and bright and hot in the sky, but a cool summer's evening full of drunk bees and trivia...

Forgive me, Audrey. I hope you had around you those you loved. I hope you were cared for and cherished. Forgive me. You were never forgotten. (*He weeps.*) Oh Christ, Audrey, you wouldn't approve of these tears, would you?

Takes up pen again.

I sit here, as I have sat over the years, listening to the rain, remembering these things. They were not good years for me. Cracked years, rather, and through the cracks have crept out all the shames of my past.

THREE IMAGINED CONFRONTATIONS WITH RON

PART THREE

1ST RON   You? I forget your name but – you? Well, strike me dead! (*Laughs.*) You nearly did, didn't you? Ha! That's a joke – strike me dead! You!

You're a judge, ain't you? Remember the first time I see your photo in the paper I said I know that face. It was the eyes. Young Tom used to call you 'bleedin' clever-eyes'. There's a lot of water passed under the bridge since then, eh?

Come to see old scar-face? Come to see how 'the handsomest of plumbers' survived? Well, I can't grumble. I was scarred but I wasn't maimed. Could have lost a hand on a blow-lamp in our trade, couldn't we, or fallen off a ladder and broke me back? I'm a bit of a sight to look at, and age don't help, but I've got me health, and as you can see from me flat I ain't bad off. Blimey! You do look pale.

Tell you what. It's only the afternoon, I know, but how about a spot of whisky? What'll your blood say to that? Bring a bit of colour to your cheeks this will. The best. Glenmorangi. Spoil meself. We don't want to go remembering rotten old times. I didn't have a full life, not a full family life like others but it was a sort of a life. Even travelled a bit. Plumbed on liners to sunny places. And I've seen poverty and misery makes *my* life seem like it was spent in heaven.

You crying? You mustn't cry. That's not a manly thing to do, your honour, not for someone in your position. And what for? I didn't much cry for meself so I don't have no need for your tears.

2ND RON (*Cry of rage.*) Out! Get out! You value your life you'll get out. Out! Out! You won't? Right! See this wire brush, see it? If you're not out by the time I count three, I'll have this down the left side of your face. One. Two. Three. Out! Get out!

   His rage subsides.

You knew, didn't you? You cocky bastard, clever eyes, you knew I couldn't do it. Though God knows how you knew 'cos there's many a time I imagined meeting you or looking you up and it was only with murder in my heart, I promise you.

What have you come for? Say sorry? Offer me compensation now you're a rich and famous judge? Why now? Why not when I was in torment 'cos I knew I'd never find a wife and never have a family and me friends were gone and me spirit and me hope for things?

And how did you find me? Eh? Of course! The lords of the land have access to all things. You can look up your files and ask friends in high places.

No. It was Katie wasn't it – the woman from the greengrocer's shop? But how did you get to *her*? Oh well, it don't matter, do it? Not any of it. Life's over. When you retire life's over anyway.

No good *you* crying, mate. It's me got things to cry for. Ha! Listen to him. *He's* crying…

3RD RON Can't say I see you properly. Lost me sight, see. Had an accident made everything blurred. That's why the place is in such a mess so you'll have to excuse it. Can you find somewhere to sit in all this rubbish? I have someone come in and clean up once a week but I can't see what she does. As long as the main things are in place so's I can find me way around and there's a smell of lavender polish, I don't mind. Lavender polish! Must have the smell of lavender polish about the place.

Hilary Hawkins you say your name is? Can't honestly say I remember a Hilary Hawkins. Can't honestly say I remember anything much. Work in the legal profession, do you? What you come and see me for? I done something wrong? Funny thing, that. I tell you what I do wrong, mister, I go on living, that's what I do wrong. I go on and on and on and on, much as I'd like not to. I mean would *you* want to go on living like this?

Some old people round here I meet them sometimes and they tell me, they tell me they wake up in the mornings and they say 'Well, thank God I made it to another day'. Not me. I wake up from darkness into semi-darkness and I say, 'Oh hell!' I say, 'not another day.' I wake up and I say, 'God help me, I've got to go through this lot again.' I wake up and I say, 'Bloody Christ! The dream's over.' Every day for forty years the dream's been over for me.

What's that whimpering? You hear whimpering? Where's it coming from, I wonder? Can you hear it? Sounds like a child's crying in a corner, done something wrong and gone into the corner to get out the way of punishment. Open that door. See if you can see someone. Here, sonny! Here, little boy! Don't cry! You can't go through life expecting never to do anything wrong. Come here to old scar-face. I've got some chocolate here. You come an' tell old scar-face about it, he'll put it right. He'll tell you about the world and things. Once upon a time there was the most handsomest plumber this side of the Atlantic…

From *Men Die Women Survive* (previously *Three Women Talking*)

Synopsis:

Minerva, a business woman, was left by her husband, Montcrieff, a writer, five years ago.

Mischa, a Hebrew scholar, left her husband, Leo, a financier, two years ago.

Claire, researcher for, and the mistress of, a shadow cabinet minister, Vincent, has just been abandoned by him to pursue family and career.

The three women have come together for dinner in order to console Claire. Each has made one of the three courses and selected a wine to accompany it. Each explains the reason for their choice and in the process we hear of their relationships with their men and gradually realise that Claire has revenged herself by betraying her politician lover.

In between, an actor plays out scenes from the life of the three men.

FOUR SPEECHES OF MONTCRIEFF

FIRST SPEECH, ACT ONE SCENE TWO

> *MONTCRIEFF'S study. He seems to be talking to a young girlfriend off stage.*

MONTCRIEFF And she blackmailed me with it, my wife, Minerva. 'I had the pain you had the pleasure.' But I didn't want the pleasure, I wanted the pain. I *wanted* to have babies. Yes, my love – birth! More than anything in the world I wanted to give birth, my own children, not be dependent on the blackmailing female of the tribe.

Are you listening in there? If we're to become new partners in life you must know about me. I don't only want to give birth to a literary masterpiece I also want to give birth to a life.

What's that you say? Too late? Men can't give birth
after fifty? You're right! And didn't she know it.
'Men can't give birth after fifty' she mocked. Taunted
me with my limitations. 'I had the pain you had the
pleasure.' An emotional terrorist, my wife. Leading
light of the women's mafia. The Godmother!

SECOND SPEECH, ACT ONE SCENE FIVE

MONTCRIEFF No one was really her favourite person. Except me.
I was the centre of her life. That was her downfall. I
was wild, full of appetites and divine discontent, the
kind of man women find a challenge. Like cowboys
tame wild horses certain women are driven to tame
wild men.

(*Calling.*) Are you listening? Are you there, my
dream girl, my lucky find, my once-in-a-lifetime
lover?

I could never understand why Shakespeare created a
Katherina to be tamed by a Petruchio. Got it wrong
again didn't he? Got Richard Three wrong; got de
ole black man wrong; got the Jew wrong, oi! And
women! Except in love. He knew about love and
passion. Ah! Old Will! Where there's a will there's a
play!

But tame me she could not, my ex! 'Frivolous!
Infantile! Failed!' she scoffed. I am not, I hasten
to assure you, entirely failed – I do make a living
as a writer. And not entirely frivolous either. Not
English enough to be entirely frivolous. Have you
observed the neurotic drive of the English to be ever
flippant? Tiresome, don't you think? Or are you
irretrievably English? Perhaps you're not English
at all but completely, utterly, helplessly foreign! Or
English with foreign extractions? I don't really know
what you look like. Blonde? Brunette? Grey? (*Pause.*)
Black? White? Asiatic?

Would you like me to cook for you? It's true I can't
have babies but I'm a very good cook, and when
you got broody I'd get broody and I'd look after you
wonderfully. (*Pause.*) She will answer me one day
won't she?

THIRD SPEECH, ACT ONE SCENE ELEVEN

MONTCRIEFF 'The great attribute of chaos is that you can count on
it! Chaos is dependable…'

(*Calling.*) Is that *your* experience of life, my
once-upon-a-time princess? That chaos is
dependable?

> *Listens as though to her reply which gives him
> pleasure.*

There's no chaos in *you*, is there? In you is the still
centre all men crave. How fortunate I am to have
found you. And I warn you I will keep you all
to myself, tucked away in these hills, chaotic old
humanity left far behind…

My ex-darling was an archdeacon of chaos. Not her
Christmas-pudding affairs, oh no! Those were kept
in order. Her emotional affairs! Those! The chaos lay
in her emotions. Her heart produced a turbulence
the unpredictability of which had me and she and
she and me buffeted around our lives like helpless
flotsam in a gale.

Oh she told me about him, her physics professor.
She couldn't resist letting me know every pass made
after I left. One conversation with him about the
new science of chaos and she knew all about it. She
was the kind who attends a lecture on a complex
subject and overnight is an instant expert! That was
she. What I called 'a topper'! Any item of knowledge
you presumed to offer a company, she could top it.

'I see the Prime Minister has accepted an invitation
to the Middle East.'

'Ah, but have you heard his wife has refused to accompany him in protest against their treatment of women?'

'They've reached the moon then!'

'Yes. Took them twenty-seven hours and forty-three point two minutes'.

'I hear What's-his-name is going to star in Thingamebob's new movie.'

'Well that was the plan, dear, had their plane not crashed half an hour ago!'

I don't know where she got her information from. Her nipples seemed to act like antennae to the world's airwaves.

But I really didn't mind her knowing things. *That* wasn't our problem.

FOURTH SPEECH, ACT ONE SCENE THIRTEEN

MONTCRIEFF Our problem was me: I had broody longings for immortality. Babies and literature – she stood it for twenty-five years then kicked me out. And who can blame her? Babies and literature. Lit-er-a-ture!

And what is it? Scavenging! A writer is a vulture that picks at the dead and the partly living. Well, not quite. But who can deny the element of scavenging in literature? Hovering over the livers and lovers, the mad and the dying, recording their passions, picking up their mistakes, weaving patterns out of their laughter and lunacy. All my best lines are other people's, Oscar, and I make my living from him and her and a *soup-çon* of imagination the trick of which you can buy at any academic supermarket. Writer? Huh! I'm a picker-up, a pecker-off, a nibbler of this and that from here and there, an intellectual magpie, an emotional thief, a beachcomber of other people's lives. And when I've got it all down in a book I go in to a market place and I take it out of my pocket like a vendor of dirty postcards, slightly ashamed. 'You buy? Cheap and lovely literature! Best art in town! Here, in my pocket! Ssh! Don't answer too loud. No one else must see and hear.'

You think I exaggerate, dearly beloved, my darling, my dove, my heart? Although there's nothing wrong with a little bit of exaggeration, I promise you I do not.

So what could she expect me to do with love, my ex, my producer-of-vintage-Christmas-puddings-out-of-which-she-has-made-a-small-fortune? What *is* love but another sack of discarded expectations to be sorted out, selected, listed and filed for lit-er-a-ture?

He picks up and reads from one of the letters he's been folding away in envelopes.

(*Reading.*) 'Dear Jason, my new novel is about chaos…in the past…you have published…but now I think… something new, something special… Would you read…?'

Pauses to consider what he's written, sardonic and resigned.

Archivists, that's all we are, of other people's fond eccentricities, tragic errors, their lost illusions. Literature! Lit-er-a-ture! LIT. ER. A. TURE!

Are you still with me, my honey, my heart?

FOUR SPEECHES OF VINCENT

FIRST SPEECH, ACT ONE SCENE THREE

TV studio. VINCENT is preparing to be interviewed.

VINCENT Yes, I know the questions become very personal at the end. I'm one of the millions who gawp at your programme. You're quite merciless on occasions. But I think I can cope, I've nothing to hide. Though I'm not ashamed to admit, I'd sooner face my opposite in the House of Commons than face that evil eye there. How's my tie? I can never get my tie right. First the wide end's too long then the thin end's too long. I tie and untie a dozen times before they come equal. Or nearly equal. The wide end always has to be a wee bit longer, I'm aware of that. I'm jabbering aren't I? I'm aware of that too. Nerves. I'll be all right though. Once your camera's turning and you're asking me difficult questions I'll be away. This idiot you see before you will turn into an oracle, a sage and wit of the kind we in Scotland produce endlessly much to the envy and chagrin of the English who are cool, calculating and boring – I promise. Does the light have to shine so brightly?

SECOND SPEECH. ACT ONE SCENE NINE

He's being interviewed.

VINCENT There is no doubt in my mind that the three major issues to confront the 21st century will be world poverty, environment, and a conflict between believers and non-believers. Or, to be more optimistic, between countries driven by religious fanaticism and countries with a tradition of religious tolerance. But those are the chapter headings not the sub-headings, and it's the sub-headings which are crucial.

He pauses as though listening to an interviewer's question.

What do I mean by that? What I mean by that is – take the problem of the conflict between religious fanaticism and religious tolerance. Voltaire thought it was solved 250 years ago when the age of reason dawned over Europe, but reason and tolerance didn't, like spring, burst out all over. Now, why? We have to be able to identify the spiritual bacteria that inflames bigotry. Or do we just pacify religious states with a kind of soothing, there-there-we-love-you diplomacy? Is education the answer to fanaticism? Or must we make damn sure we've got a good military defence against holy wars?

Here's a formulation which I think should be printed as huge posters and stuck on walls all over the world:

> My respect for your liberty to live and pray and believe as you wish does not mean I have to respect *what* you believe, *how* you live or the *content* of your prayers.

Pause. Listening.

What? Yes. I *am* a believer, believe it or not!

THIRD SPEECH, ACT ONE SCENE FIFTEEN

Still being interviewed.

VINCENT I'm glad you've asked me that question. But I'd better warn you my reply will be controversial.

Few people know *how* to behave as equals. They either want to dominate or be subservient. It's a fraught problem, central to relationships between priests and their flock, politicians and their adherents, capital and labour, men and men, women and women, men and women!

Equality is a Queenly concept we all love to love because it flatters us. But she's not an easy lady to comprehend. Consider: if you place a simple mind alongside a wise mind and declare them equal in the sight of God you will at once intimidate the simple mind. It can't compete. If you place an *aggressively* simple mind alongside a wise mind that is totally *without* aggression, and declare *them* equal then you at once intimidate the wise mind. The one can't handle wisdom, the other can't handle belligerence.

Look at the problems between men and women – and I think we should because I believe the 21st century will be the century of the woman – though not without a kind of emotional bloodshed. Most women – and many are not going to like what I say, and I may be losing myself their votes but not too many I hope because I'd like to think I appeal to those who vote for honesty rather than demagogy – but most women seem not to *want* to behave as equals! They either want to dominate or serve. There may be historical or social reasons for this, but I'm not a sociologist, I can only describe my experience of those relationships.

We are here dealing with an uncomfortable concept. Most men and women in their relationships do not eye one another as potential partners but as potential combatants. The question they present to themselves is not 'do I love?' but 'can I win?'

FOURTH SPEECH, ACT TWO SCENE TWENTY ONE

Still being interviewed.

VINCENT If I were Prime Minister? I'm not sure that's the sort of question I should be answering. On the other hand I long ago decided – and our leader accepted this when I was invited to take up the post of Shadow Minister for Environment – that I was not going to tailor my personality to a political career. My political career would have to tailor itself to me.

Party policy you'll find in manifestos drawn up by committee, but a party leader is flesh and blood. A myriad of idiosyncrasies – idiosyncratic habits, idiosyncratic tastes, idiosyncratic thoughts. Now, I'm against the cult of personality but I can't be bland! I can't fade into an anonymous background.

So, if I were Prime Minister I'd want the people to be in no uncertainty as to the kind of person I am. They should know what I think, believe, fear and even doubt. Especially my doubts. I mean – there are a lot of very important issues to be considered: the eternal cycle of injustice, revolution, injustice, revolution…for example; the relationship of education to liberty; the role of envy in human conflict. It's not enough for a leader of a party to be good at putting pennies on a tax here and taking them off there – what's the quality of *thought* behind the decision, that's what *I'd* want to know.

So, if I were Prime Minister I'd set up a chain of key lectures. Say four a year. And my priority themes would be: The Individual Spirit – does capitalism release or shackle it? Second: Human Nature – good, evil or irrational. Third: The Decline of Language and its Relationship to Inhumanity. Fourth: Violence to Achieve Ends – the vicious circle.

FOUR SPEECHES OF LEO

FIRST SPEECH, ACT ONE SCENE ONE

> *A garden. LEO is professionally strong and able but emotionally adrift.*

LEO (*Calling.*) MISCHAAAAAAAA.

> *He has hauled out a lawn mower from the shed and is confronting it like a strange beast he's never before encountered.*

*He seems to remember you need to pull out a choke.
Does so. He next remembers the pull-start. He jerks
it once, twice, three times, to no avail. He sits, easily
defeated, exhausted, bewildered.*

*A thought, like a slowly gathering storm, is assembling
in his mind.*

The universe is a ball
bounced by a child
living on a planet
placed in a universe bounced
by a child
living on a planet
placed in a universe bounced
by a child
living on a planet
placed in a universe bounced
by a child
living on a planet...

He finds the image a gloomy one. He looks up.

You gave me that, Lord. Don't blame me.

*His thoughts, his memories overwhelm him. He cries
out again –*

MISCHAAAAAAAA!

*Takes control of himself. Speaks to his wife rather
than the Lord.*

Sorry. You don't like shouting. I know. Forgive me.

I'll get over it. Don't worry, Mischa. Husbands
survive desertion. We're left bruised but we survive.
Only it takes time.

I remember, you used to ask me: 'What one,
unexpected thing would you like to do in your life?
You're a financial analyst for a big stockbroking
firm but what,' you asked, 'is the one secret thing
you've really always wanted to do? Something *really*
surprising.'

And I never knew what to reply. Used to drive you mad, I know, but what could I do, Mischa? I just didn't have a secret ambition. Forgive me.

Softer.

Mischaaaaaaaa!

SECOND SPEECH, ACT ONE SCENE SEVEN

He's at the lawn mower again which still refuses to come alive.

LEO Gardeners! Why do employees fall ill?

Cups hands to his face and again cries out to the air in desperation –

MISCHAAAAAAAA!

Long silence. He calms down.

She stopped loving me, what could I do? Stopped! Ceased! Dried up! Childhood friends, thirteen years married, two children and I became unlovable! Unloved any longer. Like this lawn mower. Though this lawn mower I never loved.

It's not a crime – to stop loving me. To stop loving me I could not say with my hand on my heart was heinous. It's everyone's right to love, not to love, to love less, to stop loving.

But of course it was not so simple, because she liked me, perhaps even more than liked me. And why not? I was a good man – faithful, loyal, dependable! I'd given her the best years of my life, her beloved children, days of roses and wine and verse beneath the bough. Why shouldn't she like me a little, even a lot?

But love? That searing madness? That insatiable longing? That absurd thrill of one finger on a cheek? That ache to be there all the time? That sharp nerve-end sharing of every domestic detail of the day: she watching him peel her an apple,

him watching her drying her skin, she watching
him shaving, swimming together, walking together,
listening to music, watching a movie, just holding
on to one another for the dear last years of life?
None of that. All that dead and gone. Affection in
place of passion… Sad… Sad and over… Batteries
run out… Sing lullabies for the day's end… Sing
lamentations… For the night has come…

THIRD SPEECH, ACT TWO SCENE SEVENTEEN

> *LEO – his lawnmower – three more attempts. Fails.*
> *Sits.*

LEO

> The universe is a ball
> bounced by a child
> living on a planet
> placed in a universe bounced
> by a child
> living on a planet
> placed in a universe bounced
> by a child…

> *It is his private incantation, his secular rosary. But it*
> *is not really what is preoccupying him.*

> *Slowly, working it out, almost word by word…*

The real difference between men and women is
that women have the perceptive power to *recognise*
paradise when they see it, the emotional capacity
to hang *onto* it, and the confidence not to care
whether paradise wants them or not. Men are never
certain it's *paradise* they see. That's why she stopped
loving me – she'd seen paradise. A man who she
knew – without the slightest, the merest, the merest,
the slightest hesitation – she was in love with. And in
she zoomed!

'You', she said, 'do not support me either
emotionally, intellectually, or in bed. You suffer
from,' she said, 'constipation of the imagination.'

And she was right! I was dead! I only came alive in business conferences. What was wrong with me, was *me*!

What could I do? Stopped loving me! Ceased! Dried up! Unloved any longer. I had become – unlovable!

FOURTH SPEECH, ACT TWO SCENE TWENTY FIVE

Sitting on a bench. Disconsolate.

LEO Let us contemplate suicide.

First problem: how? Armoury? I do not possess. A knife in my heart? My hands would be unable to push. Sleeping pills? I would fall asleep before taking enough of them. Gas? She cooked by electricity. My car? Ah! My car! Close garage doors. Sit. Switch on. Breath deeply. A comfortable way to go.

Second problem: why?

Long, long pause.

Third problem: A will. Is my will made out? Of course. Do I want to make changes? None. Are all my affairs in order? All!

Pause.

Return to problem two: why? Everyone is interesting.

Pause.

Even when they're boring they're interesting.

Pause.

But not for as long as those who are *not* boring.

Pause.

And *I* am definitely boring. I *am* boring! I am *boring*!

If I stop and try to make my mind think something interesting, I can't! Look! I sit here and squeeze and squeeze, like trying to get juice from a shrivelled up old orange and –

Hold for a long pause as he tries to fill his mind with something to surprise himself.

– I can't! Nothing comes! Only if I think about – my job – my profession. *That* excites me – the flow, the placing, the reproductive mechanisms of money. I can't help it! Money excites me. Why should I be ashamed of that, Mischa? It helped you, your family, our friends.

Thinks about this.

Oh God! I'm so boring I bore myself. It's an illness. I need help, treatment, I need pity. Pity not derision…

MISCHAAAAAAAAA!

Hardy. I need Hardy. Must phone Hardy. He doesn't think much of me but he'll help. For old time's sake. I'll phone him now. (*Rises.*) I don't really want to die. I want to be loved. I do, I do. Loved… Looked after… I'll provide the money, somebody look after me. There must be a cure for an affliction like boringness.

Pause.

Is there such a word – 'boringness'?

Exits, calling…

Hardy, Hardy, Hardy…

ACT ONE SCENE SIX

MISCHA's apartment.

MISCHA Before I began translating the *Song of Songs* I wanted to visit the land where the cedars come from… Ernest Renan who, as you probably know, was the eminent 'membre de L'Académie française' and wrote a celebrated Life of Jesus, also put forward the theory that the *Song of Songs* is not really a long poem by Solomon but a kind of play *about* Solomon. About Solomon and a Shulamite shepherdess who was *abducted* by Solomon when he saw her tending

the vineyards one day. Far from loving Solomon
she's really very unimpressed with him and longs for
her true love who is a shepherd. Says Solomon to his
Shulamite:

> 'Thou art beautiful, oh my love, as Tirzah,
> comely as Jerusalem ' –

– and then he adds 'terrible as an army with
banners'. Now why does he add that? Why does he
tell her she is as terrible as an army with banners?
Renan thinks the answer lies further down in verse
twelve of chapter six.

> 'I went down into the garden of nuts to see the
> fruits of the valley and to see whether the vine
> flourished, and the pomegranates budded.'
> 'Or ever I was aware, my soul made me like the
> chariots of Ammi-nadib.'

Oh fatal step! A visit to the vines, and there she
was – lifted into the chariot of a king's train.

MISCHA plonks wine on the table.

Red wine from Lebanon. Kosraia '64!

Solomon made himself a chariot of the wood of
Lebanon. His palace was in Lebanon. The shepherd
tells his Shulamite love: '… and the smell of thy
garments is like the smell of Lebanon… 'So, I had
to see Lebanon. The tiny village of Kosraia, in the
south, a lush, hilly area called Alboukah…

I'd been walking all morning, before the sun became
too hot, and had to stop in a restaurant for a coffee
and a mid-morning snack. The restaurateur was a
little man who spoke Arabic, French and English.
We began talking. And when I told him that I was
making a new translation of the *Song of Songs* in the
shape of a play, to my surprise he asked: from which
language – Hebrew or Latin? I told him, Hebrew.
'You're Jewish?' he asked. 'I'm British' I said, 'but
a Hebrew scholar.' 'You're Jewish,' he said, 'don't
be afraid. We all have our madmen. I'm not one of

them. Here,' he said, and he took out a plate from
his rusty, peeling old fridge, 'here, a taste you will
never taste anywhere else in the world. I had it from
my parents,' he said, 'who had it from their parents
who had it from their parents all the way back to
Seulemen – Kibbey Nayeh.' I give you the recipe,
sisters: fresh raw lamb, minced; crushed wheat; raw
onion, cut small, crisp; one beaten egg; Arabic sweet
pepper; salt; and a local herb impossible to buy
here called Kamoun. I begged it from a Lebanese
restaurant in Piccadilly.

> *MISCHA pours out the wine. They raise their glasses
> to each other, drink, then turn their attention to 'the
> dish'.*

Taste!

ACT ONE SCENE TEN

> *MISCHA's apartment.*

> *MINERVA lays out her three fondue sauces. 'Lights'
> the paraffin. Pours wine for them.*

MINERVA The bastard left me but he knew how to cook, and
petty will I not be. The fondue, sisters, is the first
meal he ever prepared for me and though I hate and
despise his frivolous and infantile spirit yet will I
honour his culinary memory.

You have before you one red, one green, one yellow
sauce, these being the traditional colours of the
fondue meal. My red is sour cream, reddened with
a tomato paste, heated with a touch of cayenne
pepper, chilli and some drops of Tabasco. My
green is mousse of avocado with créme fraîche
and drops of lemon. My yellow is as much to do
with textures as tastes – mayonnaise which I made
myself, mandarin slices – from the tin I'm afraid,
and crushed walnuts. Sweet, crunchy, velvety, and
softly fatty. On the small plates you will find raw
mushrooms, raw onion, and slices of green pepper to

spear with your beef which is – I promise you – best fillet no expense spared.

The wine comes to me from other sources and marks the end of my marriage. Between this fondue and this red wine stretches, sisters dear, a quarter of a century of married bliss and blood. Could a graph be drawn it would show a steady decline from the heights of unimaginably original passion to the lows of unbelievably original venom. By the end we were lacerating one another into emotional cubes which, like the meats we are about to deep-fry, we deep-fried in our very own and seething blue angers.

The details are banal, and just as banal was the fact that I loved him throughout. Until he left me. Then I hated him. To go through all that pain and misery and not reap the pleasures of hate? Not this sister, my sisters. I could forgive the bastard not.

Pause. Waiting for a sign.

And do I hear you ask me *how* I discovered the wine?

MINERVA tells her story as though reading from a novel.

He stood me up for a concert one night. It was Bernstein conducting Mahler. Sold out. A man was looking for a ticket. An American professor of physics. I sold him mine. We sat alongside each other saying nothing. Both of us afraid the other would mistake a word for a pass. Mahler flooded our emotions. At one moment I dared to glance at him. His eyes were closed. Ah! The sensitive soul I thought. Until his head thumped loose on my left shoulder. Jet lag! Here was a boy needing to be tucked up in bed not ravished by the chords of Jewish melancholy. I reassured him with the most sympathetic of my famed smiles. In the foyer he caught up with me.

'Could you direct me,' he asked with that special brand of mournful American courtesy, 'Could you direct me to the nearest Underground?'

'Where are you making for?' I, with absolutely no intention of taking him there, responded.

'The Westbury Hotel' he replied with the appeal of a lost and lonely visitor to strange lands.

'I'll take you there,' I said, weakness overwhelming my poor old woman's resolve.

On arrival he said: 'Whenever I come to London, which is at least four times a year for conferences and the theatre, the first thing I do is go to Berry Brothers at number Three St James Street, Piccadilly, to buy six bottles of good wine and one bottle of superb wine. In my room I have,' he continued in low, dark and confidential tones, 'already decanted by room service one hour before my expected return, a bottle of 1955 Château Margaux. Thirty years old, brown in colour and with an immense aroma of age and wisdom and utter, utter confidence. Will you,' he asked as though it was the last dance and he had finally plucked up courage, 'will you join me if I promise, hand on heart, to behave and advance you nothing but the story of my life?'

Fearing and hoping he would break his promise I accepted. We drank this wine-from-another-planet and he told me that he was researching – wait for it – 'chaos'.

'Chaos,' he revealed to me, 'is the new discipline raging through and binding together all the disciplines of science which,' he informed me, 'during the last half century have been peeling away from one another into specialist corners.'

Did you know, sisters, that all is chaos in the physical world out there?

'Far from discovering a law and order to all things as Newton predicted, nothing,' he was rivetingly dramatic about it, 'nothing happens in quite the same way twice. We are victims of,' and here he introduced me to one of the most tenderly formulated notions I've ever heard so harken to it, sisters, 'we are victims of 'the sensitive dependence on initial conditions''. I'll repeat it for verily is it lovely: 'the sensitive dependence on initial conditions, a phenomenon known as: 'the butterfly effect' which is,' he informed me, 'the notion that a butterfly stirring the air today in Peking can transform storm systems next month in New York. You hit a storm, you can feel it, but who will ever know which butterfly was where, that caused it? Chaos!' he warned me, 'all is chaos.'

And when he asked me what *I* did I found myself weeping as I described how my husband had nagged me for years to found a business of vintage Christmas puddings and how I had resisted and he had been right and I became successful and now we lived in a state he glorified as his 'divine discontent' but which you, I and all the world knows was blood, tears, and yes, chaos! I had told no one till then. The Château Margaux, assisted no doubt by Gustav Mahler, had released my confession and – here's the point – revealed the possibility of reconciliation. But, when I returned home, I discovered – he'd fled. Yes. Fled! Men don't leave, they flee – guilt in their hearts, terror and chaos up their arse.

Beware of the red sauce, sisters, it's hot!

ACT ONE SCENE SIXTEEN

CLAIRE   He was, he was! Vincent was generous, able,
dynamic company, an adequate lover too, but he
was – oh, that special brand of put-downer. There I
was – high on being the researcher and mistress of
a shadow cabinet minister but – not a week went by
that he didn't talk about the brilliant, erudite talented
women of the past – George Eliot, Beatrice Webb,
Virginia Woolf… A marvellous heritage of women,
true, but Vincent beat me with them, the greats of
the past, as though he himself was one of those very
greats. And he constantly laid upon me facts he
knew I'd not be able to contradict. He didn't do it
maliciously, oppressively, there was no spite in the
man but – I don't know. It was as though he didn't
know how to behave as an equal. He *talked* about
equality, talked like one who *believed* himself your
equal. But he seemed incapable of *behaving* like one.
Perhaps I *wasn't* his equal – he was after all a very
capable man: astute at political assessment, shrewd
at human assessment, quick-witted, good memory,
widely read, social graces and – something I admired
in him more than anything else – intellectual
courage, he took risks in his career, but – it was
essential to his self-confidence that someone was
around twenty-four hours a day to reassure him
that he was superior, not by word but simply by
being. I was that being. With me he could be benign,
generous, modest, helpful, over-flowing with advice.
I made him seem wise to himself, allowed him
to bestow bounty, permitted his magnanimity to
blossom.

   Her tone changes.

And I loved every minute of it.

Ah, moral Mischa who imagines she's found her
knight in shining armour, her prince Charming.
Do you really think me shocking and degraded?

Performing the service of making him appear wise
and superior had the reverse effect of making *me* feel
wise and superior. Permitting him to assume control
simply meant *I* was in control. Do you think I *really*
considered him wiser than me? As the servant who
deferred, as his admirer who bowed I was able to
manipulate him for my own needs… And do you
think I *loved* him? That I even like men as a species?
I – have needs, they – provide. They fuck my
appetites away and I can command high salaries…

For that I must dissemble a state of mind allows
them to imagine *they* are in control. But oh are they
not! And *you* know they're not. Between ourselves
let's be honest: men are for manipulating… Why
else were we given tears?… And sighs and soft
curves?…

And what about eyes? What *can't* be put into eyes,
tell me? Like bottles you can fill at will with different
colours, so with our eyes – vessels to be filled with all
those glorious shades of emotion. Gaiety one minute,
vulnerability the next. A touch of melancholy here,
a hint of longing there, the wicked brilliance of
passion, the damp ducts of helplessness, the milky
hue of modesty – whatsoever emotion is required for
our ends we can call up into our eyes, and few men
can resist.

And let us not, sisters, let us not talk about our
sexuality. That would be giving too much away,
wouldn't it? You, Mischa, ask can we be honest
about men? You, Minerva, say there'll be no
pussy-footing around this table? Right! Recall the
moments, those splendid moments of total control,
when you've stood naked and become triumphantly
aware of the power in each moulded part…when
you've isolated each magnetic mound and known
its sensuous weight in gold… There you've stood,
knowing how the allure of breasts drew hands.
There you've stood, knowing that mound at the
base of your belly drew hands. And that belly – oh

I knew what drew my teenage lover to stroke and circle the palm of his hand round and round and round and round... Nine out of ten women wouldn't admit it, but for most there was at least one time in their lives when they stood before a mirror facing their flesh and aware that every voluptuous part was bewitching, delicious, magnetic! The curve of a neck, the long soft side of their arms, the down of a thigh, hips to be held, buttocks to be squeezed, fingers and toes and nipples to be sucked. Power! Pulsating, intoxicated, confident, through every nerve-end – power! The tool we must learn to handle for delight and the security of our lives – power! The power to bestow that one deep and excruciating pleasure that all men helplessly crave – it's ours! And with it we have them, malleable, for manipulating – men! Deny it if you dare, sisters dear! Contradict me if you dare, sisters dear! Talk to me of love if you dare, dear, dear sisters, dear!

ACT ONE SCENE EIGHTEEN

CLAIRE   Something light. A cheesecake. A lot of calories – I know – but – light. Fluffy... And... Tokay. From Hungary... I ate it first time in – Auschwitz...

> *Long pause.*

Polish members of parliament invite British members of parliament to visit rebuilt Warsaw, beautiful Cracow, the ski slopes of Zakopane, and Auschwitz – obligatory... I didn't want to go. I hate confrontations with suffering, feeling helpless, weeping tears I haven't earned...

I saw a grey-haired old woman staring at me. She held a plastic carrier bag in her hand, which made me think she was a local. I nodded to her, and she spoke to me. It was quite a shock, actually. She had a heavy Polish accent tucked inside a heavy American one.

'You're not going to *visit* are you!' she said. She didn't ask, she stated. She seemed to know. 'I see many like you,' she said. 'They come to the gates but they can't go on. I don't blame them. *I* only come', she said, 'because my family is here, and if my family wasn't here I wouldn't come either.'

And she told me this story of how her entire family – parents, brothers, sisters, uncles, aunts, cousins and grandparents – all! Gassed! She survived because she was the clever one and the family saved up money to send her to study in Paris. And it seems her youngest sister, in the midst of all that deprivation, used to save crumbs to feed a baby bird she'd found.

'So I come every year to feed birds and visit my family'.

Which made me weep…

And to console me this grey-haired old woman fed me her home-made cheesecake. 'Here,' she said. 'It's my own recipe. And I've given it a name.' I asked her what name? 'Five-thousand-years-of-suffering cheesecake,' she replied. Which made me laugh. We both laughed. Imagine – feeding birds, eating cheesecake and laughing at the gates of Auschwitz!

ACT TWO SCENE TWENTY TWO

MISCHA The truth about paradise is this: the serpent was Jewish!

Leo was obsessed with the thought that paradise lost was the cause of conflict between men and women. Men can't forgive women because Eve seduced Adam into biting the apple, which lost them paradise. But he missed the point, my poor Leo. The conflict is not between men and women over the fall from grace, it's between men on one side and women and Jews on the other. 'Get thee with learning,' whispered the Jewish serpent. 'Bite!

You'll see better!' *He* knew a useful tool when he
saw it. So Eve, being a woman with an instinct for
the good things in life, and having more courage
than her male companion, bit, and got pregnant
with learning, and lost paradise! For all of us! (*Pause.*)
Been hated ever since. (*Pause.*) Oppressed and hated.
(*Pause.*) Jews and women! (*Pause.*) For knowing too
much.

I read in the paper the other day that a woman got
off for murdering her husband because he beat her,
for long periods, cruelly, until she couldn't stand
it any longer. And the occasion when he beat her
most was when she used a word with more than one
syllable. 'Don't you use educated words with me,'
he cried at her. 'Don't you come the clever stuff
with me. Bam! Wallop! Bash! Take that and that and
that!' (*Pause.*) Women and Jews. (*Pause.*) For biting an
apple. (*Pause.*) Funny old life.

ACT TWO SCENE TWENTY SIX

> *The Puzaltski story. All funny stories rely upon the
> teller. We write it out here but the actress is at liberty
> to restructure it to her own style of telling, like a solo
> violinist given free rein in a cadenza.*

CLAIRE   Puzaltski was the fourth reserve of a famous
American football team. So famous that it always
had star players and poor Puzaltski was never ever in
fifteen years called on field to play a match.

Retirement is upon him. Comes the last Saturday in
his career, he wakes up, sits down to his breakfast of
steak and french fries and says to his wife –

> *– In a heavy 'Brando Waterfront' accent.*

'Dat's it! Finished! I'm not going to de match!'

His wife is aghast.

'You're not going to the match? The last match! It's
unprofessional not to play the last match!'

'Don't tell me!' cries a deeply unhappy and humiliated Puzaltski. 'But for fifteen years I've been fourth reserve and I ain't never ever been called to play a game. Fifteen years sitting on de side-lines. Do you have any idea what it's like only ever to sit on de side-lines and never be a player? What kinda life was dat?'

'Maybe today,' says his wife, 'today they'll call you!'

'Dey haven't called me in fifteen years, why should dey call me on my very last day wid de team?'

His wife is fearful.

'You skip the last match they'll cut off your retirement pension and then where will we be?'

'I'm not going and dey won't cut off my retirement pension and we'll be OK.' Puzaltski is adamant.

'*I'll* go!' cries his distraught wife. 'I'll take your place!'

'You?' laughs her husband. 'You're a woman!'

Mrs Puzaltski ignores him.

'I'll get to the locker room early, I'll get into all that gear – who'll know?'

'It won't work.'

'It'll work! I'll just be a number sitting on the side-lines and I won't say a word. Did anybody ever talk to *you*?'

'Never!'

'So – it'll work!'

And away she goes. Locker room. Changes. The coach puts his arm round her and pats her on the bum. Sits on the side-lines. First half of the match, as always, the team remains intact. Then, second half – chaos takes over! Down goes one player. The first reserve is called. Down goes a second payer. The second reserve is called. A very nervous Mrs Puzaltski is sitting on the side-lines.

CLAIRE begins to titter.

(*Carefully.*) It is a game she does not know how to play!

As the story progresses all three women will gradually be drawn in to infectious laughter even before the punch line.

Fifteen minutes before the end of the game the home team is losing, the fans are not very happy. Then, the unimaginable happens. A third player goes down and the cry goes up for the fourth reserve. 'PUZALTSKI!'

There's no way out. She has to go onto the field.

CLAIRE enacts it.

There she is, bending down, looking around, understanding nothing, praying she'll be called upon to do nothing, and the numbers come. Out of sequence. Meaningless. Fast. Nine! Seven! Three! Five! Two! Wham! She suddenly finds the ball coming her way. She catches! She runs! Of course she doesn't know what *should* be done so she does the right thing in the wrong way. A crazy dash. While she runs with the ball the players jump on each other. Touch down! The fans go wild.

Who is this guy? They've never seen him before. The name is whispered. The whisper spreads and soon the name is on everyone's lips.

'Puzaltski! Puzaltski!'

Meanwhile Mrs Puzaltski is a very bewildered and frightened woman.

'This is not,' she says to herself, head bent down, 'a very wise thing to have done.'

The crazy numbers begin again. Different ones. Two! Nine! Seven! One! Ten! She understands nothing, but there again – wham! The ball's in her hands. She runs. Unorthodox. Another touch down! The field's in confusion. The fans are delirious. They're chanting:

PU-ZALT-SKI! PU-ZALT-SKI! PU-ZALT-SKI!

Meanwhile the other side are getting very, very worried indeed, and they get into a huddle.

'I don't know what the fuck's happening,' says their captain, 'but one thing's for certain – we gotta nail that guy they call Puzaltski!'

So there they are again. Heads down, numbers flying, and every eye of the enemy team on Mrs Puzaltski who by this time is beginning to enjoy herself. Five! Three! Seven! Two! Eight! Wham! The ball's in her hands again and in a flash eleven men are on top of her. She's out! Cold!

Next thing she knows she's in the dressing room, stripped, and the trainer is over her pushing down at her breasts as though trying to get them to be somewhere else. She opens her eyes and it's obvious – she is amazed! The trainer bends over her full of admiration and reassurance and he says:

'Ya did good Puzaltski, ya did real swell. And don't worry about a ting. I'll have ya right in no time. As soon as I getcha balls back into place your prick will come out of hiding!'

From *Blood Libel*

Synopsis:

This is the story of the first ever 'blood libel' accusation. *

In 1144 a young boy was found brutally murdered in Thorpe Wood, Norwich, England.

The cry went up that it was the work of the Jews who had slaughtered a Christian child to use his blood for Passover and mock the crucifixion.

The Prior of the Norwich Priory, Elias, did not believe the accusation and the charge was dropped until some twenty years later the monk, Thomas of Monmouth, joined the priory and took up the cause to have the boy William honoured as martyr.

He and the zealous monks of the priory had their way; a special tomb was set up; pilgrims came in search of miracles and the church grew rich.

William's death would today be acknowledged for what it almost certainly was in the 12th century – a crime of sexual assault. Blood Libel acknowledges this while playing out the myth of martyrdom – a contrapunction of furious irony.

Again the theme of the dangers of religious dogma and fanaticism.

ACT TWO SCENE THIRTEEN

> *ELIAS, Prior of the Church of Norwich, aged 60, is talking with DON AIMAR, Prior of St Pancras.*

ELIAS   A martyr is not a martyr unless he die for his religion. Not suffering but *why* he suffered is what lays claim to martyrdom… The boy William was murdered, I strongly suspect, by a mad and cruel stranger for cruel obscene desires of the flesh…It cannot be proven it was the Jew… Besides, such spilling of blood goes against their teachings… It goes against all reason. The Jews have no normal freedoms here. They're the property of the King

---

*A calumnious accusation that Jews murder Christian children to use their blood for baking unleavened bread – matzot – to celebrate the Passover. A calumny which has spread throughout Europe and persists to this day.

who taxes them at a whim. They're clever and rich for both of which they're hated and resented. They're small in number – *three* thousand. Why should they risk such crimes?

Somewhere you will read that to drink dried menstrual blood will induce the menstrual cycle, that to eat three lice between bread will cure colic, that to prevent the bursting of a dam a child must be buried alive, that to immure a human being in its foundations will ensure the building stands.

And if you read the books of early Christian sects you will find *them* full of blood rituals, the sacrifice of babes and the eating of their parts. Whereas turn to Leviticus, turn to Deuteronomy and you will find such sacrifice most strictly forbidden to the Israelites.

The ecumenical councils pass edict after edict declaring such belief in Jewish slaughter false, yet such belief persists. I am tired of the ignorance and stupidity of the simple flock. The simple flock chooses superstition for which it needs no learning. I am tired, yes, and full of contempt. Jesus was a Jew steeped in the knowledge of the wisest laws. Law, learning, mercy, wisdom – these are the pillars of the Christian faith. They represent all that I cherish in this damned existence, they are the only hope for hopeless mankind, they are what formed my life and what in life I informed. I will not bow to the fevered intoxications of illiterate monks who love more their image before God than God's meaning to the world.

From *Wild Spring*

Synopsis:

Gertie, aged forty-four, an actress at the peak of her career, adopted a child, Tom, who turned out to have Down's Syndrome; she's recently befriended the young black theatre car-attendant, Sam, aged nineteen.

He's bright but hooked to a self-deprecating image of himself as a born car attendant.

Gertie is successful but flirts with the image of herself as someone more useful than a mere actress. Sam falls in love with her but she resists. Each tries to argue the other out of the fond images they have of themselves. Act One ends with the death of Gertie's adopted son.

Act Two, fifteen years later, Gertie's career is in crisis. She's in love – unrequited – with Kennedy, aged thirty, the black company manager who has a fond image of himself as an artist but who in fact is a born entrepreneur.

Acting as a metaphor for the false images of ourselves with which we fall in love.

The two men need not be black but can be any kind of ethnic outsider.

ACT ONE SCENE TWO

> *GERTIE's dressing room. Sound of applause. The play has ended. GERTIE, petite, pugnaciously pretty, enters from the room where she has been de-robing, only the 'Fool's' cap on her head remains from her costume. The rest is underwear. She is buoyant, bubbling. Pours herself a whisky. She talks to her unseen dresser, LOTTIE, in the other room through which comes a general backstage buzz.*

GERTIE My God, didn't they love all that tonight. A woman playing the Fool! They'll go home and tell their family and friends 'do you know, the Fool was played by Gertie Matthews, a woman! Fantastic!'

> *In front of the mirror.*

Sharp! Sharp, sharp, sharp!

To LOTTIE'

That's it, Lottie. I won't be needing anything else.
Don't hang about. See you tomorrow.

*Closes door. Turns down tannoy. Starts to take off
make-up. Singing.*

'When that I was but a tiny little boy
With a heigh-ho the wind and the rain…'

No! Stop that Gertie! You can't carry the play around
with you everywhere. Leave it alone, on stage, wash
it out of your hair.

Singing
'I'm gonna wash ole Shakespeare out of
my hair
I'm gonna wash ole Shakespeare out of
my hair
I'm gonna wash ole Shakespeare out of
my hair
Gonna send him on his way.'

(*Closing her eyes.*) If I close my eyes I can see
everything that's wonderful about being alive.

You're in good spirits tonight, Gertie. What's
happened? (*Beat.*) I'll give you three guesses. (*Beat.*)
You've been asked to take over the company. God
forbid! Confront actors' egos all day every day?
(*Beat.*) You've discovered your mother is not really
your mother, you were adopted. Ha! Wouldn't
that change my life. (*Beat.*) You're going to be laid
tonight. Wrong again! That would put me in very
high spirits indeed, but all the men are dead as far
as I can make out. Or emigrated. (*Beat.*) What, then?
(*Beat.*) I'll tell you what then, you were stunning
tonight, that's fucking what then. You were one
hundred per cent in tune with your Fool and you
knew it and they knew it and you knew they knew
it, and they knew you knew and they loved you and

you loved them and everybody loved everybody
and it was electric and fantastic. Fan-fucking-tastic.
(*Beat.*) Gawd! That's terrible! To be so dependent
upon praise. To be so dependent upon the praise of
an audience for your happiness – that's a shameful
confession. Just a little love and admiration from
anybody and you're anybody's!

Make-up is off. Contemplates herself in the mirror.

'You walk like a crab' said my ballet teacher when
my mother took me to classes aged eight. 'I hope
you don't dance like one.' *Do* I walk like a crab?

She stands and walks, slightly sideways.

I suppose I do. But not on stage. On stage, Gertie
Matthews, you're something else. Crab off stage but
on stage – goddess!

Knock on her door.

Enter!

ACT ONE SCENE TWO

*SAM looks around. He loves the atmosphere of dressing
rooms.*

SAM   She trusts you, Sam. You could pinch her watch
which she's forgotten. (*Pockets her watch.*) You could
steal this antique coffee cup which'd fetch a bob
or two. (*Pockets cup.*) I bet this old print is worth
something. (*Slips it into his overalls.*)

(*Imitating her.*) 'My mum made *me* a liar because
she didn't let me go out with the friends I liked, so
now I lie like a chameleon. But you and me' – She's
always talking about her mum. 'My mum was
a manipulator…' 'What's a manipulator, Miss
Matthews?' 'My dad was hungry for affection but
my mum was emotionally parsimonious…' 'What's
'parsimonious', Miss Matthews?' 'Gertie hasn't got
looks, said my mum, but she's got character…'

She has, too. Aren't you lucky I like you, Miss Matthews? (*Returns print.*) Aren't you lucky I'm your friend, Miss Matthews? (*Returns cup.*) Aren't you lucky you can trust me, Miss Matthews? (*Returns watch.*) I've got a mum, too, and she tell me 'You steal, boy, and you end up messing your only life. And don't think 'cos I'm your mum I'll come running to bail you out, 'cos I won't.' So, Miss Matthews, we both got mums.

> *He says it in such a way that we're not certain.*

(*Closing his eyes.*) If I close my eyes I can hear my head thinking.

> *He places the Fool's hat on his head. Preens himself. He's no actor but he's heard the lines many times.*

> 'This is a brave night to cool a courtesan –
> I'll speak a prophecy ere I go…'

'You steal, boy, and you end up messing your only life.' Good ole mum.

> *He makes a joyful leap in the air kicking his feet together.*

You enjoy being trusted don't you, Sam boy?

> *Another leap. Sound of applause. Taking off hat, he bows.*

ACT ONE SCENE THREE

> *An award ceremony.*

> *GERTRUDE stands before a microphone clutching a statue. She's crippled with embarrassment to have won.*

GERTIE   Well. What do I say? I know – that's what everyone asks: 'what do I say?' and then everyone thanks everyone. And I do. Everyone. Thank them… Oh dear – you can tell I didn't expect to win, I'm not prepared. Bit strange really. This. Such a coveted award. Just for playing the Fool. I should have lots of them if that's all it takes.

Waits for laughter.

I don't know… I'm…I'm… honoured. You all know that. It's more than honour though, isn't it? If we're truthful it's also vindication. Your work and your faith have been vindicated. You've proved them wrong. Them! Those loving doubters. My mum, bless her, she meant well, but my mum used to say 'Gertie hasn't got looks but she's got character'. 'Character'. So, I win awards playing the Fool. Ha! Yes. Well. Vindicated. And justified. You hold something like this in your hand and you feel your existence is justified. As though you've earned the air you're breathing. I'd better stop now – I'll get even sillier or weep. Thank you.

Offers an unexpected, sweet curtsy.

ACT ONE SCENE FOUR

GERTIE's dining room. She and SAM have just had lunch.

GERTIE   Well mums are always a good standby for off-loading blame. Problem with my mum was she taught me to blame myself. For everything. 'Don't annoy people, don't contradict them, don't ask favours, don't lose your temper, don't complain, don't bang doors…' She made me feel I had to apologise for the air I breathed.

She was tiny. Very tiny. And strong. Gave my poor dad a rough ole time – worked for a boot and shoe factory as a commercial traveller. Hated it. I only ever saw him when he came home at weekends so Mum and I went twice a week to the pictures and I spent the rest of my time imagining I was Doris Day or Marlene Dietrich. They were second cousins, you know. Mum and Dad, that is, not Doris and Marlene. Dad thought she was a saint. Not

Marlene, Mum. She only married him to please *her*
mum. Mum's mum, that is, not Marlene's. (*Beat.*)
You do know who Marlene Dietrich and Doris Day
are, don't you? Mums! 'The only person in the
world worth loving is your mother.' Subtle! Never
entertained the possibility you might meet someone
else. And as for sex. 'It's all disgusting, and women
never enjoy it!'

Books? *Books?* There *were* no books in the house.
You weren't supposed to *read*. I joined Boot's library
and read under the bedclothes with a torch. No
books, no conversation, no social conscience, no sex.
Just guilts. There was so much I shouldn't do that I
did and lied about, it was such a don't-do-this-or-that
upbringing that I was riddled with guilts. And
so if anything goes wrong I know it's me who's
made it go wrong. You may have noticed – I walk
like a crab, as though there's always something to
avoid. You're lucky. You're black. You can blame
everybody for everything. I've got no one except
myself to blame, at which I am an expert, believe
me. So you stay a car park attendant, Sam, you can
blame a car park attendant's life on a whole number
of things. Cosy. Try to be something more you might
fail then you'll have to blame yourself. Not so cosy.

ACT ONE SCENE FIVE

A beach.

GERTIE   When I close my eyes (*She does.*) I can see Palmers
Green. The tiny, dreary, two-up two-down behind
the curtains of which, wrote the poet, are people
living out their lives of quiet desperation. I don't
think my mum knew she was doing that but when
I close my eyes I can smell the acrid smell of the
kitchen range which she'd painted silver. She *was*.
Quietly desperate. Nothing pleased her. She found
joy in no one and no thing.

There *was* a time when she got excited. The early
days. When I close my eyes I can see dad frantically
making props and mum sewing on sequins for my
first dress in my first public appearance – Miss
Milligan's Dancing Display. But there was this girl
called Renée Harmer, 'the Harmer Girl', and when
I close my eyes I can hear mum saying 'if only you
smiled like the Harmer girl. Renée Harmer is so
pretty. You watch the Harmer girl *she'll* go places.'
Practised like the furies but it wasn't enough for my
mum.

When I close my eyes I can see photographers
flashing. I can see Mum taking my make-up off
with margarine. I can hear the compliments of
anyone who was anyone in North London. And
all ending, every Saturday, year in year out, eating
raisin-sandwiches and drinking cocoa.

When I close my eyes I can see my dad painting.
Landscapes. That's all he wanted to be – a landscape
painter. He was a dreamer with never enough talent
to make his dreams come true but just enough sense
never to wake up.

When I close my eyes I can see every blister like a
medal, feel every headache like tokens of triumph.

> *Long pause.*

What do *you* see when you close your eyes?

ACT ONE SCENE FIVE

> *A beach.*

SAM When I close my eyes (*Closes them.*) – hills. Purple
hills. Behind me. In front – a beach. All sand.
No stones. No stones and no people. I'm lying
flat on my back. Bermuda shorts, pattern from
playing-cards – red diamonds, black spades, red
hearts, black clubs. My eyes are closed. Suddenly – I
feel a snake. Crawling over me. Up my leg, my

sides, under my armpit. It stays there. Curled-up and
snug. I'm terrified. Can't move. Can't open my eyes.
Hours pass. Hours and hours and hours. It's night.
I can hear the tide getting closer. And closer. And
closer. Water's touching my feet. Covering my legs.
I've got to move. I've *got* to. I move. The snake bites.
I die.

Long pause.

When I close my eyes – screaming. Dad beats
Mum. Mum beats Sister. Sister beats me. I beat
brothers. Blood. When I close my eyes – blood
and screaming. No one listens. No one to no one.
Screaming. Blood.

When I close my eyes –

With eyes closed he struggles.

When I close my eyes –

Struggles more.

When I close my eyes –

*Struggle turns to distress as though he were an epileptic,
which he's not.*

When I close my eyes I'm all feeling. Can't see
anything really. Can't think anything either.

He thinks about this..

'Where you going, Mum?'

'Out! Away from you bloody lot.'

'Don't go, Mum. I'll keep them quiet.'

'What, this brood? Quiet? Not till hell freezes over'.

'Where you going, Dad?'

'Out'

'Out where?'

'Just out! Anywhere but here.'

'Don't go, Dad. We'll paint the living room.'

'You all give me grief, you know that? Grief!'

Everybody loved everybody, only nobody loved
themselves.

ACT ONE SCENE EIGHT

TOM's bedside. GERTIE's there.

GERTIE   I'm sorry, Tom. Some things I could do for you,
some I couldn't. Some things I can help, some I
can't. But Mum will look after you. That's what
mums are for aren't they, to look after their children,
be there, run around for them? And there's no
doubt I run around for you. Got me running around
all over the place haven't you, on the end of your
little string? I shouldn't let you do it, you'll grow up
spoilt and impossible. You're not very possible now,
are you, poor ole fellow? God made you only half
possible. Wonder why he did that? Got tired halfway
did he? Do you think he did that with most of us?
Got tired halfway? Feels like it sometimes, that I'm
only half made. It's alright when I'm up there on the
stage being wonderful and loved and admired, but
there's the rest of the time.

Still – the rest of the time is you, isn't it? Thank God
for you, Tom. Acting and looking after you go well
together. There's only half of you and only half of
me which makes a good fit I'd say. Wouldn't you?
So don't close your eyes, Tom, stay awake with me.
I need you. To fit the other half. You'll make him
stay won't you, God? I mean, I know you work
in mysterious ways, but don't be too mysterious.
Not all the time. I mean – give yourself a break,
throw a little light on things now and then, I've got
to understand something... Don't be mean about
meaning, there's a good God.

ACT ONE SCENE NINE

> *Rehearsal room. GERTIE has just rehearsed Gertrude in* Hamlet. *(Act 3 Scene 4)*

GERTIE   You thought that was my best so far, did you?
Yes, well I'm feeling a little sad today, perhaps
that helps. (*Listens.*) Oh, nothing serious. Just one
of those days. It'll pass. (*Listens.*) What a strange
question. Of course I know that there's more than
one way to deliver a line. Every actor knows that.
(*Pause.*) But to tell you the truth, now you ask, I'm
not certain. I think, oh dear, I'm not sure I can
say this, you'll disagree violently, but I have this
horrible suspicion there's probably only *one* right
way to deliver a line and all the time we're struggling
to find it – that one right way. And we think each
time we do it differently, each time another actor
is doing it differently, that we're giving a different
'interpretation'. But we're not. It's not really
interpretation is it? We do it differently because we
can't *help* doing it differently – we are each of us
different and in our different ways we're struggling
to find the one right way to deliver it, to get the line
into focus. A bit like life, actually. Never succeed of
course. Life's always out of focus, isn't it? But that
doesn't stop us aiming for focus, the one right way.
(*Pause.*) Can I tell you a story – perhaps it's time for a
break?

> *She may or may not sit on a chair.*

I was at a dinner party once, not theatre people
but – others. A mixed crowd – writers, business
people, media – and I happened to say to my
neighbour at the dinner table just what I've said
now, that there's probably only one right way to
deliver a line. And this neighbour, a businessman,
turned abruptly on me and said '*Well I think that's
the biggest load of nonsense I've ever heard*'. Rude and

abrupt. No discussion, just insult. It hurt I can tell
you. So I shut up. Went silent. Sulked probably.

And the hostess could see something was wrong
so she asked what had happened. And the whole
table went quiet and turned to us. Terrifying. But
I thought: I'll try something out. And I told them.
'This man,' I said, 'this gentleman on my right here,
we were having a discussion about acting and I put it
to him that there was probably only one right way to
deliver a line, and he said –

She imitates an exaggeratedly apologetic man.

'Well I think that's the biggest load of nonsense I've
ever heard'. At which he protested, saying 'No, no! I
didn't say it like that. I don't have a pathetic nature.'
'Oh, of course,' I said, 'you said it like this':

*She imitates an exaggeratedly loud and aggressive
man.*

'Well I think that's the biggest load of nonsense I've
ever heard'! At which he protested again. 'No, no! I
didn't say it like that either. I don't have a belligerent
nature.' 'Oh, I'm sorry,' I said. 'Do you mean there's
only one right way you delivered your line?'

*She allows this to sink in. Despite the intensity of
her anecdote her mind is elsewhere. The 'director' is
questioning her.*

(*Listening.*) Yes, something *is* wrong. Tom is dying.
Leukaemia.

(*Listening.*) Yes – in *very* mysterious ways.

ACT TWO SCENE TWO

GERTIE's dressing room.

She's in a state having dried many times during her speech.

KENNEDY is attempting to console her and feed her food and drink.

In one hand she holds a glass of wine and is trembling.

GERTIE   … Can you tremble like that? You think I am just acting.

Pause.

'Just acting'. Are you aware, Mr Phillips, that society normally uses the name of our profession as a term of abuse? 'Oh ignore her, she's just acting!' Are you aware, Mr Phillips, that every night I go out there in front of an audience and pretend to be who I am not? Are you aware, Mr Phillips, that if I did that in public-life I'd be shunned, vilified, called a humbug, a fraud, a sham, a fake, a liar, but up there, made-up, lights bright, someone else's words of wit and brilliance, I can dissemble to my heart's content, it's acceptable, no one gives a toss. What is despised in a person *off* stage I am deceiving an audience into praising *on* stage. And the more convincingly I deceive the more they praise. They even pay for it. Are you aware of all that, Mr Phillips? Audacious, huh? What other profession do you know where the professional exposes herself to the ridicule of disbelief, the ignominy of dismissal, the humiliation of being seen through, and makes that her *raison d'être*, her justification for existing, eh? What other profession?

Her make-up is off. Her face is 'naked'. She pulls her hair to stick up, defiantly making herself unattractive.

Come to bed. I have such delights to offer you…

Why *do* I dry as Lear's Fool? What *is* there about
that speech?...

It's not just the drying it's the fearing. And it's not
just the fearing, it's the fearing of fearing. It's the
putting yourself up there when the 'believe-in-me' is
gone. Everything goes out of your head. Your body
is paralysed. Terror! It's to do with being caught
out. If you dry then everybody suddenly knows
you've been 'just acting'. Blood drains from you and
in its place shame seeps like poison through your
whole system. I've often stood in the wings and
thought – I'm not going out there. I can't do that
show again tonight. And I've wanted to lock myself
in the dressing room. And I think – when will that
day come, locking myself in – when is it going to be
me?

Long pause. Mood changing.

Ha! there was this actor who'd made up a set of
seven lines for when *he* dried in a Shakespeare role.

> 'Aye, my Lord, yonder Hereford cometh
> And Shrewsbury too. And York hath mounted
> And will shortly come. Behold is yonder
> Basingstoke your favourite forsooth
> And Cornwall calls thee home to rest.
> Look Sire, Somerset and Dorset too
> And Surrey, aye, and Buckingham...'

By which time he'd either remembered the lines or
his colleagues had fed him.

Both are convulsed.

ACT TWO SCENE TWO

GERTIE's dressing room.

KENNEDY My mum? Married at seventeen, had five children, and when the youngest was fourteen said goodbye to us all and went off with a dark stranger. It was as if she'd just been given the charge of us for a short while until the time came to give us back. Though who to, we never found out. She rings one of us now and then but we don't see much of her. Strange lady. Laughed at everything and seemed to understand nothing. When we meet she looks at us as though she's trying to remember who we are...

Dad? Poor old Dad is a very bewildered, incompetent bricklayer who works non-stop for builders with no standards. His wife going off with a dark stranger bewildered him; his children's ability to thrive and survive without either of them bewilders him; and the builders who continue to employ him bewilder him...

My people? My people? (*Sardonically.*) Which 'people'? My family 'people' or my black 'people'?...

I once got into a fight at school defending a white boy against the overwhelming odds of three black boys who turned on me and screamed, 'Where are your roots, black boy? Don'tcha know where you belong? Roots, man, roots!' To which I replied, 'My roots are anywhere intelligence resides'. Having said which they laid me out flat as on a slab for the dead... Complicated...

ACT TWO SCENE TWO

GERTIE's dressing room.

KENNEDY It so happens I'm good with money... I actually do understand money... I'll confess something – I've actually made money. I bought a house when I was 24, got a 90 per cent mortgage, sold it in the last of the boom years, made a killing and invested... And what's more, I'm ashamed to admit it but I invested wisely...

I have this gift. I can make money reproduce itself. I've always had it. Since school days. I traded. In anything. Buy from one boy and sell to another. No one knew. I always had money and no one knew how. Used to think I stole.

Sometimes when I close my eyes the language of finance floats before me. I feel as though I'm engaged with something supremely wicked, like being with a marvellous whore. Everything is possible. 'Dividend'. 'Charge account'. 'Money supply'. 'White knight'. 'Opening price'. 'Elastic currency'. 'Liquidity'. 'Open mouth operations'. 'Risk capital'. 'Placing'. 'Overnight money'. 'Order'. 'Tender'. 'Yield'. A world vibrating with challenge, stimulating the imagination, releasing energies. To buy with one hand and sell with the other, to know what to buy and when to sell, to judge what the market needs, the price it can take – it's all my language, my world.

And other times when I close my eyes another language takes over – poetry floats before me.

> And on the pedestal these words appear:
> 'My name is Ozymandias, king of kings;
> Look on my works, ye Mighty, and despair!'
> Nothing beside remains. Round the decay
> Of that colossal wreck, boundless and bare,
> The lone and level sands stretch far away.

I'm a torn man, Gertie – artist or trader?

ACT TWO SCENE TWO & THREE
(TWO MONOLOGUES LINKED)

GERTIE's dressing room.

GERTIE Ah, food. Now, if you really want to know and understand everything about me, and you *do* want to know and understand everything about me don't you, Mr Phillips, because that's the only way you'll get me into bed, and I respect you for it, you don't rush a girl, I can see that – so if you really want to know and understand me – watch me eat.

She removes the covering hood.

Have you ever watched me eat?…

Love food, hate eating it. The act of cutting things up on a plate – how do you do it without it sliding off the edge? How do you push potatoes and beans with a knife onto a fork without them falling? And when you succeed and you feel safe enough to raise them to your mouth, how do you make sure they stay there? That's my real terror, food dropping off my fork, back onto the plate, splashing the hostess's best tablecloth, or my best dress. So I lower my face to the plate which I know is wrong, you're supposed to raise your food to your mouth, I know it, and sometimes I try, surreptitiously, which is impossible because by this time I know everyone is looking at me so I get embarrassed, and hover, and my face goes down and my fork comes up, a compromise, which doesn't work because my mouth is never ever where my fork imagines it is. I once pronged the back of my throat! You wouldn't think it possible would you? An anxious face went down too far and an eager fork came up too high. Aaarrrgghh!

Feigns strangulation.

Eating is an agony when there's only one other person, at a dinner table it's a nightmare.

Pause.

Why are you afflicted thus, Gertrude?

I'm glad you asked why I am afflicted thus.

Because, Mr Phillips, although I keep baldly asking you to impale yourself upon me I am, deep deep down where it counts, a very shy and tortured woman who feels she has to apologise for the air she breathes.

Pause.

Why am I afflicted thus?

I'm glad you asked me why I am afflicted thus.

Because, Mr Phillips, of Mum – who I idolised out of all proportion until I saw she had feet of clay and then I just stopped liking her. And when I stopped liking her I lost her. Like a bereavement. My fault, really, for making her a saint. We fall in love with images *we* make of ourselves and of other people. It's never really what we are or what they really are, is it?...

Something loveable about her? Loveable? She used to polish the window-ledges outside the house. Painted them glossy white then polished them. (*Pause.*) Taught me to stand on my head in the kitchen. (*Pause.*) She wanted to ride a motor-bike. (*Pause.*) She wanted to travel. (*Pause.*) She loved Sherbet Dabs and I loved it that my mum was a friend who loved Sherbet Dabs... Loveable? Yes. She was...

Long pause.

She was also a killer... Power! That's what my mum was interested in, power! Over people's lives. Her sisters'. Mine. Dad's. She treated Dad like muck. Muck! He knew all about her but he adored her so she got away with it. Beyond the pale she was for him, even after she discovered drink and oh, did my mother discover drink! No stopping her manipulations then. Want to know why I dry? The killer still manipulates me from the grave. 'Don't you go thinking you've got talent, Gertie. It's just God's gift.' God? She didn't give a toss about God, except when she needed him on her side. Made people love her and trust her so's she could control them God-like and set them up against each other.

But not the clever ones. Not our friends. She was good with au pairs and chamber maids, had them eating out of her hand – they were inferior, see, she could control *them*. But not our friends. She went silent in front of *their* conversation. Anything she didn't understand intimidated her, so then she'd fuss around and do domestic and 'sensible' things and usually wreck our evenings.

I shall never forgive her betraying me to my aunts. Got me to confide in her then went off and told them. Killer! But she had God on her side, see, so anything I did he'd tell her about anyway whether I confided in her or not.

And why do you think she sucked Sherbet Dabs with me, loveable ole Mum? Not because she liked Sherbet Dabs, no! She sucked Sherbet Dabs with me like a ten year old in order to be my friend. Partner 'gainst dad, see. 'Buy them at the corner shop, we'll eat them in the kitchen. Ssh! Our secret. Don't tell Daddy.' 'Let's go to the cinema. After school. Every Wednesday. Ssh! Our secret. Don't tell Daddy.' What a friend, I thought. She understood about sweets and movies on a school-day. 'Ssh! Our secret! Don't tell Daddy.' Loveable? Killer!

And all that polishing of the window ledges, the order, the neatness. A trap! To make coming home impossible to resist. A terrifying killer-woman full of terrifying, ignorant nonsense, and I lived with that nonsense in terror for years and years till I was

pock-marked with don'ts and guilts and confused
messages sending me all over the place.

You know the season she hated most? Spring! A time
of growing, stirrings, wild winds. Hated it! Oh she
was a dangerous woman. One of the wasted women
of the world and there's nothing more dangerous
than a wasted woman. Killer! 'Don't tell Daddy! Ssh!
Our secret. Don't tell Daddy!'

And then I discovered I loved him. She'd kept
me from him. This dignified, deeply emotional,
frustrated, de-balled man who only wanted to paint
landscapes. Loved him! But too late. Now that's
a real guilt. I earned that one. Not like the others
which I had chained to me. Killer! I can't believe I
allowed all her malevolent nonsense to rule my life.
Killer! Killer, killer, killer!

ACT TWO SCENE THREE

GERTIE's dining room, talking to KENNEDY.

GERTIE   You want to be an actor, Kennedy, but could you
cope with rejection? That's the killer. Coping with
rejection. To be turned down for a part makes you
feel unworthy to be alive – could you take that?
'Too old, too young, too short, too pretty, too good,
not good enough, too experienced, not experienced
enough.' Still want to be an actor? If they've seen
you playing Shakespeare you don't get the Cockney
part; if they see you in the Cockney part you don't
get the countess. 'Oh, you're a comedienne!' 'Oh,
you're a tragedienne!' Still want to be an actor?

And then there are those interviews when the
director tells you 'you could play this part with your
hands tied behind your back' and you go home
elated, and a month passes and you bump into a
chum in the supermarket and ask her what she's
doing and she tells you 'I'm rather excited actually,
I'm doing…' and she lets you know she's got the job

you've been waiting a month to hear about and you
suddenly feel like a cartload of cattle. Still want to be
an actor?…

Listening.

I've heard that one before, and there's women would
hit you over the head for saying that but it thrills
me. – 'desirable when you're angry'. Tell me I'm
desirable and I'll burn up on stage. There are two
kinds of bad performance: one – due to no talent;
two – due to no sex. If a good actor is having an off
night you can bet your bottom dollar her lover's
gone off her. When I was desired I was dynamite in
performance. Tell me I'm not desirable and I enter
stage right like lead. Ambition slinks off into the
wings. I'm a dead lump. D-E-A-D, dead… Still want
to be an actor?

ACT TWO SCENE FOUR

The beach.

GERTIE Are you aware, Mr Phillips, how full the world is
of lonely women? I could list you a dozen I know.
Right now. All young to middle-aged. Professional or
capable, single, with children, full of affection, lively,
bursting to give and give and give. Lonely. Not for
friendship but for love.

Why should that be do you think? I've never been
able to fathom it out. Too fussy? Too intelligent?
Too demanding? Sexless? Do we overwhelm?
Give out the wrong smells? Do we carry years of
defeat in our eyes? I suppose that would be very off
putting – defeat. Like failure – everyone stays away.
And it's a killer. First rejection and then loneliness.

No, don't protest, there's a limit to occupying
myself – walks, art galleries, Canadian exercises,
gardening. Amnesty one day, a sick friend the next. I
do it very well, even happily, making notes to myself
about interesting radio programmes and books I

imagine will help me make sense of this…this… I've run out of adjectives to describe 'life'. Bewildering? Miserable? Complex? I don't know. Probably all of them. It seethes with everything this life. That's the word! 'Seething!' This 'seething' life, to make sense of this seething life. Even a tiny corner of it. But there's a limit. And after it I'm lonely. Desperately, painfully, heart-achingly lonely. I sometimes think I'm dying from lack of love. Loved by no one, touched by no one. Not even a child. If someone, somewhere doesn't put their arms round me in *real* love one of these days I think I'm going to die.

Pause.

See what I mean? Me me me me me! We came here to face your identity crisis.

Pause.

Or was that just your excuse to get me away from my problem.

Pause.

Why is everyone unhappy?

From *Denial*

Synopsis

About the 'false memory syndrome'.

Based on a case history of a daughter who, encouraged by the unhealthy influence of a charlatan therapist, falsely accuses her parents of sexual abuse.

She turns on her parents falsely accusing them of sexually abusing her as a child. The play, more sympathetic to the parents than the daughter, explores the nature of the therapist as manipulator.

SCENE TWO

> *The shrill voice of the daughter, JENNY, leaving a message on the telephone answer machine.*
>
> *Her delivery is fast, manic.*

JENNY'S VOICE This message is for you, Matthew, father, Matthew fucking father, to let you know that I know, I know, I now know that the man who calls himself my father Matthew fucking father was so fucking fatherly and loving that he loved me like a lover. Like a fucking lover. Ha! Does that make you smile, pet? A fucking lover?

You raped me, Matthew, father, Matthew fucking father, you raped me and then tried to give *me* the responsibility of *your* shame. Well fuck you! I'm not going to take it any longer because it's yours you fucker, you rapist of children.

Remember what you used to do to me? Shall I remind you? When I was two and you were reading stories to me at night you'd get into bed with me and use your fucking fingers wouldn't you? And it really used to hurt, it used to hurt so fucking much you bastard, you.

And then when I was four you took me to that fucking meeting where you watched, you and

granddad, you stood at the back, didn't you, you
stood at the back watching other men bugger me? I
fucking hate you, Matthew, father, Matthew fucking
father, for everything you've done to me.

But I'm over it. I'm over it and I'm never ever
gonna let you get away with it. So don't ever write
to me again, you stupid bastard, and don't ever
ever come near your grandchildren again. They're
not your grandchildren. You *have* no grandchildren.
No grandchildren, no daughter, nothing. Guilt
and shame, that's what you've got. And that's all,
Matthew, father, Matthew fucking father. I'm never
ever ever ever going to forgive you. For anything!
Nothing!

SCENE THREE

ZIGGY LANDSMAN's study.

*An old man, old friend of KAREN's father. ZIGGY and
KAREN. He's there to listen.*

KAREN   I've seen her, Ziggy. I needed to see her. It was an
ache.

My plan is to catch her as she's taking the children
to school. Quarter past eight in the morning. I drive
there and wait. I have this pain in me, this pain,
here, I have it from the moment I get up – not that
I slept, you can imagine. And she comes out of the
door with them, sees me, and – I can understand
this – she gives a scream: 'Ahhhh!' I say: 'I'm sorry,
Jenny, I didn't mean to frighten you'. 'What are
you doing here?' she asks, a bit roughly, so it hurts.
And I tell her, 'You must forgive me, Jenny, but this
mum, this mum who loves and misses her daughter
had to come and see her.'

And that's all I was going to say. I said it, touched
her, and turned to walk away. 'I'm taking the
children to school,' she says, 'why don't you get in
the car?' I can't believe my ears. She wants me to

stay with her? So, I get in the car like it's the most
natural thing in the world, and we drive the children
to school with me asking them simple questions
about their teacher and how they're getting on,
and do they like reading – nothing too demanding,
nothing too emotional.

And then I'm left in the car with her. And I'm silent.
Waiting for her. Finally she says: 'Well, you haven't
said anything about how I look.' That mass of
chestnut hair, remember it? Gone! She'd cut it down
to a crew cut. Shocking. But all I say is: 'Oh, your
new hairstyle…'well' I say, 'you've got a beautiful
face so it doesn't matter what hairstyle you have.'
'Yes,' she says, 'that's what most people say. It gives
me freedom,' she says. So I say to her, gentle as ever
I could: 'You know, Jenny, freedom doesn't come
with a haircut.' She says nothing.

After a while she begins spouting at me. Her jargon:
'People have to get in touch with their anger, their
inner child…abused children have been robbed
of their childhood…' That sort of thing. And I let
her go on, and I'm thinking all the time of that
childhood, that wonderful childhood, that time of
parties and friends all over the place, and holidays
here, there, and everywhere. And I think 'robbed'?
Funny word.

For two hours I sat in that car, listening, till I think
to myself now it's my turn. And I begin. 'Jenny,' I
begin, 'when you were running the new-age shop
your favourite cousin came to see you with her
children that you'd never seen – why couldn't you
speak with her?' She doesn't answer. 'Jenny,' I say,
'your sister, Abigail, she could never be bothered
to celebrate her birthdays, you always organised
them *for* her – you loved her. Why have you broken
contact?' She doesn't answer. 'Your grandfather,
Jenny, you adored him. He's ill, he asks after you,
phone him – what will it cost you?' She doesn't
answer. 'And me,' I say to her, 'think about *me*, think

of the kind of mother *I* was – would I ever have allowed anything in my home? Remember,' I tell her, 'you only get one mother. That's all you get, just one. Think about it.' 'I will,' she says. 'I'll talk to my therapist and think about it. Perhaps,' she says, 'we can all meet together'. 'That would be wonderful, Jenny, I say.' 'I'm not promising,' she says. 'No promises.'

Freedom? She can't do anything without this therapist knowing. She shaves her head and chains herself to a therapist. Funny freedom. It makes sense to you?

And as I leave, this terrible pain, here, it's in me, a tightening. I can hardly get to my car.

SCENE FIFTEEN

The chaotic study of SANDY, journalist who has covered many such cases.

MATTHEW has come to her for advice.

MATTHEW Your first feeling is horror. Like your doctor tells you you're terminal. It's difficult to grasp. One day you've got a life ahead of you, no final fence in sight, the next – the fence has been fast-forwarded. You're over the other side. With the doomed ones. One minute you're a functioning family, your daughter's at the end of a phone talking, listening, sharing – the next, she's a stranger and you're an outcast. She's an accuser and you're on trial. Those agonising doubts: what did I do? What could I possibly have done? And then – when you can't find anything really heinous to cause such a rift you forget about yourself and you start thinking about your child. My daughter – if she's made such dreadful accusations she must be dreadfully unhappy. My agony can be nothing compared to what she must be going through. Poor Jenny… (*Holds back tears.*) Incomprehensible. We were such a happy family.

How can happiness cause such misery? It makes no
sense to me. A *happy* family.

SCENE FIFTEEN

SANDY responds to MATTHEW's speech.

SANDY A happy family! Fatal! Worst thing! Few encounters
more dispiriting than those with happy families. Let
me tell you a story.

She's trying to change his mood.

One day last year my eldest son, thirteen at the
time, was standing outside his school talking to some
friends. He's a big lad – long hair, bright, confident,
and with those irritatingly happy eyes. Two boys
approached. One kicked him in the backside the
other told him to get stuffed. He ignored them. That
really irritated them. They called to him again. 'Get
stuffed!' This time he said obligingly, 'All right, I
will'. Which of course irritated them even more.
And one of them drew back a heavy ringed fist and
smashed into my son's right eye.

No – he's alright. A bruise, a gash. Healed now.
But it made me realise – there exists a certain kind
of mean mind that hates the sight of happiness.
In anyone or any form. Loathes it. Difficult to
comprehend how such a mind functions. What
could there possibly be in the nature of happiness
to arouse such hostility, such a demonic desire to
destroy it? 'Because it's not *mine*'? 'I hate them being
happy because *I'm* not happy'? Could it be that?
Does one person's happiness highlight another's
failure? Is that it? Too dazzling? 'Stars must fall! The
mighty laid low! The achievers denied! The whole
God-blessèd edifice of joy brought down to ease the
pain of my miserable, insignificant life. How dare
you love your parents when mine were unloveable?
How dare your eyes sparkle with confidence and

happiness? Happiness? You want happiness? I'll give you happiness.' Wham!

And so it begins – the murderous, insidious, dismantling of your cherished kith, kin, and hearth. Bit by painful bit until you're made to feel guilty for adoring those who gave you birth, those who nourished you with affection, watched over your fevers, reassured you through lean doubts. So it begins.

SCENE TWENTY ONE

MATTHEW confronts the therapist.

MATTHEW   Please, don't raise your voice to me, Mrs Morgan. That's not quite 'it'. I have something I want to say to you... It's a confession of guilt... I bit their bums... Yes, I bit their bums...and it gets even worse...We *both* bit their bums. Even worser – we let them bite our bums. Jenny's right – we tampered with her. We used to have bum-biting days. The girls would run away and hide and we'd go after them, and when we found them we'd bite their bums. Then *we* would hide, and they'd look for us and when they found us they'd bite *our* bums. And everyone squealed, and everyone shrieked. Got hiccups from shrieking and squealing, and laughing and fearing. Clothed, of course.

And my worst of worstest confessions. I loved, absolutely loved bathing them – splashing them, squirting them, blowing bubbles for them, and then – rubbing them in with baby oil. Rubbing their poor little chapped thighs and groins with soothing oils. And as I did it I lingered over it, and looked into their eyes and kept bending down to kiss them. Their face, their belly, their fat arms, their toes. This little piggy went to market, this little piggy stayed at home, this little piggy ate all the roast beef, and this little piggy had none. But this little piggy

went inky pinky ponky poo – and we tickled them.
Tickle, tickle, tickled them. Terrible – no? Oh, we
tampered with them all right. And I tell you what,
Mrs Therapist, give me back their childhood and the
young man I once was and I'd have those glorious
bum-biting days all over again. All over again.

Tell me, Mrs Morgan, where were you trained?

From *Break, My Heart*

Synopsis

A working-class couple – a carpenter and his wife.

Maeve has outgrown her husband. She has discovered Shakespeare and poetry, which she learns by heart and recites to herself. Michael is intimidated by her new persona. His impoverished swearing sharply contrasts with Shakespeare's language. Maeve wants to find a job, get out of the house. Michael's pride forbids her. 'I don't want people to think I can't support my family.'

Each time she uses what he considers a long word he beats her. After each act of violence he is filled with remorse and she has to comfort him.

The cycle of beating and remorse seems never-ending.

SCENE THREE

>*MAEVE's attic hideaway.*
>
>*At her desk-top – composing and typing a 'sonnet' to her husband. .*

MAEVE

>'Shall I compare thee to a Cadbury's box?
>Thou art surprising with each bite I take.
>Thy many centres do my passions rouse
>While my own centre moistens sweetly for thy sake.'

>*Recounts the last line.*

>'While my own centre moistens sweetly for thy sake.'

Twelve beats there, Maeve, should be ten – fourteen lines of ten beats each. Iambic pentameters. Pa-dum pa-dum pa-dum pa-dum pa-dum. Try again.

>'Your many centres do my passions rouse'… er…
>'Your many centres do my passions rouse…'

>*Struggles.*

'While my sweet centre moistens for thy
sake…'

No.

'While *soft* my centre moistens for thy sake.'

Good. So –

'Shall I compare thee to a Cadbury's box?
Thou art surprising with each bite I take
Thy many centres do my passions rouse
While soft my centre moistens for thy sake.'

Is he surprising with each bite? And does your soft
centre moisten for his sake? (*Beat.*) Does your poor
soft centre *moisten*?

And why should it make him smile anyway? He
won't know the original. Can't say you married a
man who shares your 'cultural framework' can you?
And why not, Maeve, why didn't you marry such a
man?

Because you didn't have a cultural framework when
you married, did you, lovely? Didn't know your arse
from your tit when he and thee were first acquent.
All bonking, lager, and Punk Rock.

She dances as she did aged 17.

Except he wasn't even a punk. Too much colour.

The banality of the movements amaze her.

What did we think we were doing? Bit like a fast
march gone wrong. One two three four, one two
three four, left right, left right, left right, left right.

'Shall I compare thee to a summer's day?
Thou art more lovely and more temperate…'

Savours the words.

'More lovely and more temp-er-rate…
Rough winds do shake the darling buds of
May,

And summer's lease hath all too short a date.'

Considers this.

You're thirty and seven months, Maeve, nearly half
your summer's gone. (*Beat.*) The lease is all too short.

From *Groupie*

Synopsis

Matty Beancourt, a 61 year old woman, reads the autobiography of Mark Gorman, a famous painter. Having grown up in the same East End streets, she writes to him. A correspondence develops. She visits him unannounced, and discovers that far from living in fame and luxury he lives in near poverty and neglect.

Her personality is sunny, his is curmudgeonly. Their impact upon each other is startling.

ACT ONE SCENE ONE

MATTY is composing a letter to MARK.

MATTY 'Fifth of April nineteen ninety-eight. Dear Mark Gorman, I just had to write to you after reading your autobiography *Treading On Eggshells*. Nice image if I may make so bold. But then you're a painter so you *would* think up nice images wouldn't you?

'I'd borrowed it from the library and thought you'd like to know there's such a long waiting list I had to *buy* the book in the end. How brave to have written it. I felt I was being told secrets you hadn't shared with anyone else.

'I hope you don't mind another letter on top of the dozens you receive every day. Who's this one you must be thinking? Well, I was a sort of neighbour. We were kids in the same Stepney streets: Brick Lane, Spitalfields Market, Itchy Park, Bishopsgate… I lived there till I was eighteen, you moved out when you were ten otherwise we might have met.

'See why I had to write? Oh, dear. As I'm typing this I think I'm going to cry. I feel such a twit. Wait a minute, let me turn off my CD player.

'Where was I? Oh, yes – your book, your glorious book. The similarity of events, so uncanny. I *also*

learned to swim in Goulston Street baths. *And* I
played knock-a-down-Ginger. *And* I played truant
from school. *And* I had an embarrassing moment
like you getting lost and doing a pooh in your pants.
We were playing 'up the wall' and I did a handstand
and one of the boys shouted out *"look, she's got a hole
in her knickers"* I think that was the beginning of my
blushing days. Or did it begin when I played "you
show me yours and I'll show you mine"?

'Cor! She does ramble on you must be thinking. All
these words and she hasn't begun to tell you half she
wants to tell you. You don't think she's being rude,
do you? She feels as if she knows you. My husband
used to tell me I see things that aren't there. But
more times out of ten I was right.

'Good night, Mr Gorman. Mr Mark Gorman.
Mr Mark Gorman RA. Yours sincerely, Mathilda
Beancourt, or Matty – which is what close friends
call me.

'PS Of course I know your paintings as well. Rushed
to The Royal Academy half way through reading
your book and managed to buy postcards. Not the
same, though, is it? I bet you're thinking she doesn't
really know my paintings if all she knows me from
are postcards. You're right. But she can't afford
the real thing, can she? That's always been her
problem – knew the real thing, just couldn't afford it.
Mind you, I've got a little something squirreled away
for a special event – trip up the Nile, something like
that.

'PPS. You're right. The woman rambles.

'PPPS Why don't they hang you? Funny expression!'

ACT ONE SCENE THREE

Another letter from MATTY.

MATTY   'Good morning, Mr Gorman. It's the twelfth of May,
and here I am again. What a thrill. I did and I didn't
expect a reply. I didn't because, well, the famous are
famous. And I did because your autobiography told
me you would.

'I almost didn't send the first letter – frightened of
appearing stupid. Then I woke up this morning and
saw a watery sun and I thought – the spring's trying
to make it so I should, too. And I went out and
bought two hyacinths, and the scent's all over the
place.

'I won't bother you for long. Promise. But like
you I suffer from nostalgia. Loved reading about
the old Jew who played records in his battered
old baby-pram. I used to pass him on my way to
Toynbee Hall for piano lessons. You wrote that
he played records of Yiddish songs whereas I
remember them being operatic songs. Scratchy
voices and wowing violins. Well, that's memory for
you.

'And Prince Monolulu, the black betting-tipster. *"I
gotta horse! I gotta horse!"* I used to go listen to him
every Sunday when I went to buy my mum's
bread – lovely hot and crusty bread that was. I
can smell it now as I write. And those thick fogs,
pea-soupers we called them. Enough!

'I could go on and on about all sorts of things – my
dad being a policeman; my eighty-three-year-old
mum living on a police pension; Aunt Shirley who
married Harry the Jew, and the rumpus *that* caused
though not with my mum who once worked as the
secretary to a Jewish school on the Whitechapel
Road, and we think, my sister and me, that she fell
in love with Mr Cohen who ran it.

'Forgive my typing and spelling, won't you? I was never much cop at English. Piano was my first love. Gave that up long ago when I became a wife and then a mother and now I'm a granny baby-sitting my grandchildren, which is what grannies are for I suppose. Love it, actually. And I manage to go to concerts whenever any orchestra or pianist bothers to come to Milton Keynes. So I really do have a smashing life compared to some and I've gone on for too long I know.

'Finished now. Really. Goodbye. Yours sincerely Mathilda Beancourt, or Fatty Matty as I used to be called at school.

'PS Thank you for bothering to read this drivel. Of course if you threw it in the bin after the first sentence then you didn't read this drivel and I didn't need to thank you.

'PPS Beancourt is my maiden name, by the way – a Huguenot name. You probably know, most Huguenots got rich from the weaving trade and moved out. We stayed poor and stayed in! Heigh-ho! There's some as is and some as ain't. And some as do and some as don't. And some as stand and some as faint. And some as will and some as won't.

'PPPS Got any exhibitions coming up?

'PPPPS Hope I don't come over stupid.'

SCENE EIGHTEEN

MATTY writes to MARK after they've spent the previous day at the National Portrait Gallery.

MATTY 'Twenty fifth of October nineteen ninety-nine. Oh, Mark. I can't sleep, I can't read, I can't sit still, I can't stop thinking about everything you said. Everything *I* said! You made me surprise myself. That's such a great gift – to make people surprise themselves.'

Piano.

'It's in my playing, too. The notes are no longer
mechanical. And those paintings I chose! They're
in front of me as I write. Only postcards, I know,
but they remind me what I felt when I was looking
at the real thing. That's what you do – make me
feel in a way I didn't ever think I would feel again.
Most women learn to live with numbed feelings.
Husbands think they're frigid. Not true. They're just
sleeping. That's what the Prince Charming story is
about – not bringing the dead alive but making the
frozen feel. *Feel!* I'm feeling again. I never thought
I'd feel again. I can't get your face out of my head,
I can't stop the sound of your voice, I can't stop
singing "Down Mexico Way". And – hear this,
Mark – I can't stop smiling. I walk in the street and I
feel people looking at me because I'm smiling. Like
a mad woman. Smiling, smiling.

'Now, I have a proposal to put to you. Don't get
angry…'

From *Longitude*

Synopsis

In the early eighteenth century the inability to find longitude led to such loss of life and cargo that English Parliament passed an act offering £20,000 to anyone who solved the problem. Isaac Newton knew a clock would solve it but did not believe such a clock could be invented. Scientists focused on the lunar solution.

John Harrison, a carpenter and joiner from Lincolnshire, taught himself to mend clocks. He invented a land clock that ran accurately, and set himself the task of inventing a clock that could run accurately at sea. He spent his life perfecting it and, together with his son, fulfilled the tests required by Parliament.

For complex reasons the complete prize was never awarded to him. The play traces a lifetime's conflict between uneducated genius and the establishment. An epic play in a Hogarthian setting calling for music – Harrison was also a choirmaster.

ACT ONE

HARRISON What were it about me? They called me 'strange'. Strange? What were there strange? I made clocks. Taught myself to make clocks, what were strange about that? True, I didn't accept payment. Not in the beginning. But that were because I weren't easily content wi' what I'd done. Nowt strange about that. 'Obstinate'? I saw wrong and said so and kept saying so and will always keep saying so. Wrong is wrong not obstinate. Honour is honour not obstinate. Justice is justice not obstinate. It were them were strange and obstinate. Priests and professors. Them!

　　Long, reflective pause.

Nay. Not them. Me. I didn't know my place. You're not born with rights, others must bestow them. Know your place, be humble, presume nothing. I learned none of that.

Pause.

Did I presume? I built something changed men's fortunes – were that presumption?

Pause.

Nay. I presumed nothing. I *earned.* What I built *earned* me rights. I used my brain and brawn, and carved myself a place. Bestow me nothing, I said. I've earned. I wanted no bestowing, and told them so.

Pause.

And lost. Didn't know my place. Wasn't humble enough for them. Stupid man!

Pause.

Be fine when I'm long dead and gone and out of trouble's way, when they don't have my bluntness and gruffness and impatience and contempt of them grinding their ears. But alive? While I'm still around to argue back and disagree and write pamphlets 'gainst their mischievousness? Difficult! Presumptuous! Troublemaker!

Pause.

Bloody priests and professors.

ACT ONE

Harrison's workshop.

HARRISON   And then – along comes a ticking thing in a box invented not by a priest or professor but by an uneducated carpenter. A ticking thing in a box! Ha! A clock! Oh my goodness deary me. Tick tock tick tock! A clock! Oh deary deary me. Tick tock tick tock!

Do I have regrets? Were there words wrong I uttered? If I'm ill-used is the fault mine? It's beholden upon me to ask – are there other ways I could have behaved?

Considers.

I've proposed laws for music and argued that a note pitched even the tiniest degree off those laws will sound ill, not truly sweet. And I must wonder – is there in life a tone of speaking that is also not truly sweet if not pitched according to the same laws? Perhaps I didn't tune myself sweetly enough to be listened to. Perhaps, though time has *obsessed* me, I'm *out* of time. I've made clocks accurate for land and sea but perhaps nothing tick tocks accurately in me. I must ask these things.

Considers more but not for long.

Nay! Nay nay nay! I began sweetly and honestly and trustingly enough until they abused my trust. They spout nonsense whereas my clocks, I make bold to say, my timekeepers for longitude are the most beautiful and curious mechanical things in the world, and I heartily thank Almighty God that I have lived so long as in some measure to complete them. So –

Burst of choral music.

Sing out you weavers! Sing out you smithies! Sing out you shoemakers, printers, carpenters and boys. Sing out!

ACT ONE

HARRISON   Then, sir, it's about time you did hear talk like that, for if this goes on…if you prevaricate…more ships will wreck themselves upon rocks and more women and children will be made widows and orphans… Obstinate you call me, obstinate? Have none of you any idea how long it will take to prepare written descriptions and working drawings of the mechanisms and then, *then* make two watches?

And I know too well *why* you want me to do it. Yes, sir, I do, sir. Indeed I do, sir. While my timekeeper is dismantled and out of function your priest and professor the very very oh so reverend Nevil Maskelyne will seek a trial of the lunar-tic method with its mad and cumbersome measurements between fixed stars and a crazy moon. And you'll love that, all of you. Your little heads will look up and gaze at the magnificence of the heavens and you'll imagine God is speaking to you, telling you the way, and it won't matter if there's a cloud or two or three or four you'll wait till they're passed and waste time calculating when all you need is my little piece of machinery. But no! Oh no! Too vulgar for you. What's a little metal, a few springs, and tiny wheels compared to the stars? Good Lord and little fishes! Who is this upstart from up north with his tick tocking cogs and balances?

Well I'll tell you who I am. I'm John Harrison from Barrow-on-Humber, and I'm seventy years old, and I've given half my life to solving the one problem could make this country the greatest maritime nation in the world, and you little men with your tawdry conditions for this to be done first and that to be done first and everything to be done first before I receive my just rewards, you little men of theory – you're squeezing the blood out of my last years. Oh, yes. I know only too well why you want my timekeeper dismantled.

ACT TWO

HARRISON   I'm a thorn in their side. Nothing will please them but my death.

Well die I won't. I'll hell not die. I know all about
them as glory in the end of things, the passing of this
and that. *He's* had his day, they say with sadness in
their voice and glee in their dried up hearts. Expect
no more from him. His days are ended, done! Well
pass I won't and end I won't and more there is, and
they can *choke* with glee for I've got oak and God
and cleverness where they've got naught but three
chins and a shiny arse. Oh, yes, I know such men.
Beware of them, William lad. They'll drain joy from
a nightingale, dampen your sun, and lay waste the
best in you. But not in this carpenter, not in this
clockmaker, not in this bell-ringer.

Don't ask from whence but I've got energies and
fires in me to last ten lives and ring them all to hell.

From *Phoenix Phoenix Burning Bright*

Synopsis:

Two couples share a warm Whitsun holiday together in the Cambridgeshire countryside. Karl-Olaf, an historian, is spending a post-graduate year in Cambridge with is wife, Janika, a social worker, and their two children. They are from Denmark.

Raphael, professor of history of art, and one time senior lecturer to Karl-Olaf, together with his wife, Madeau, are visiting the Danes.

The days are balmy, and are spent eating, cycling, lazing in the sun, and conversing.

Karl-Olaf and Janika are having matrimonial problems. Raphael is going through a crisis of political belief, with Madeau anxiously looking on.

ACT ONE SCENE SIX

> *A pause during a cycle ride.*

JANIKA   I have this dread of something awful about to happen. It's not a fear of the bomb, I don't think it's that, but some kind of anarchy. A break-up of patterns of behaviour. I hoard things, like Christmas wrapping which I fold away neatly in drawers. And string and brown paper from parcels, plastic bags – I've got three plastic bags full of plastic bags! And there's this cupboard full of imperishable goods – tins of soups, baked beans, stewed meat, packets of tea. Two weeks' supply.

  But that's not the kind of hoarding I really want to do. What I really want to do, and I'm ashamed to admit it, is dig a huge square hole somewhere, line it with cement and plastic, and fill it up with tins of vegetables and broths, jars of pickles and Nescafé and honey and salt and spices and sugar and flour and packets of candles and batteries and vacuum flasks and soaps and medicines and bandages… For what? A siege perhaps, some unspeakable disaster. I fear – I don't know – a time of aberration, a great lapse of human kindness. They say it's the disinherited who will claim justice. Well… maybe… but I fear old scores will be paid off and new injustices made. There are such mad angers about and they frighten me and I want to lay low until they're spent, and protect my children.

ACT ONE SCENE SEVEN

In a car on the way back from an evening meal in a restaurant.

RAPHAEL Awful man! Loud mouthed, patronising, a kind of hearty bully. I once saw him, after the News. There'd been a competition and the prize was an opportunity to run around a supermarket with a trolley and pack as much into it as you could in three minutes. The winners were a middle-aged couple, kindly-looking, holidays in Southend, or Blackpool for a treat – though God knows why we look at people and presume to know them so well, but we do, and there it is. And suddenly, on the word '*go*', this timid pair from West Ham – I assume it was West Ham because it was a Sainsbury's in West Ham – suddenly this sweet, unassuming pair were immediately turned into the greediest, graspiest, grabbingest couple on earth. It was shocking, everyone egging them on, encouraging them to haul and snatch as fast as they could. 'Only two minutes left! Only one minute left! Ten, nine, eight, seven, six…' They became so excited, their arms reaching up, reaching down, their faces showing panic if they hesitated and a second passed without them having thrown some 49p or 29p or 9p article into their racing trolley. And when they'd done, to applause mind you, this gross Cockney with his hateful bonhomie triumphantly announced to the millions of viewers that the reward for this obscene display of greed, this demeaning, self-abasing race, was £124

and 46 pence worth of groceries, or thereabouts. A
month's supply of goods in return for entertaining
the crowds with the spectacle of their humiliation.
And do you think it was over? Not by half.

He had to have a go himself. To see if he could beat
them. Which of course he did! But beside him the
middle-aged couple appeared civilised. He, our
huge huggable one didn't merely 'reach for' with
honest hands, no! He flicked! This fat man ran and
flicked at things which, because they weren't bodily
lifted, more often than not knocked other things
down. Eggs smashed, bottles crashed, boxes burst
open, and he took his corners so swiftly that neatly
piled 'special offers' came tumbling down in what
for the crowd was hilarious disarray. Think of it!
His pillaging drew applause from the onlookers. In
this age of widespread poverty and anarchy he left
behind him a trail of disorder and waste and, for
me, despair. And those who watched, applauded.
Imagine! Applauded!

ACT ONE SCENE EIGHT

The study, night.

*KARL-OLAF on the floor, leaning against his bookcase,
legs straight out, arms limp, head rocking, weeping. In
one hand his glasses, in another a faded brown copy
of* The Observer. *He's in a state of total surrender,
talking to* RAPHAEL

KARL-OLAF   (*Holding up* The Observer.) This! This poor girl.
What they did to her.

Pause.

Couldn't sleep. Too much food. So – came to clear
up. All these papers. Why do we hoard newspapers?
And you know what it's like when you're throwing
papers away, you read first, to check, make sure
some 'valuable' piece of information isn't being

discarded – dates, events... All nonsense, just
nonsense. A historian's illness – hoarding facts.

And I came across this. This story. This grotesquery
about a woman they'd captured in a village in South
Vietnam. Thought she was a guerrilla. Rape, torture,
terror...this poor woman...forty-eight hours...kept
her...uncertain...for all that time...not knowing what
they'd do. They had this power over her. Soldiers
with no minds, no morality. Gangsters in uniform...
capable of infinite cruelty...someone gave them the
power. And this woman, at one moment she thinks
they'll let her go, and she's happy, and then she can
see – they won't, and she terrified, and then she's
bewildered. And I can see it, you know, I can feel
it...her only life...and they don't comprehend the
meaning of that... Her Only Life...they don't care...
and she's helpless! And in the end, after all that
waiting and uncertainty and hoping – they murder
her. No pity. No justice. Only cruelty...and I've just
read it, one of the soldiers who did it, confessed...
and it makes me cry...for her, for just her – a
victim, a helpless victim. I mean – she couldn't do
anything. She was in their hands. Bastard soldiers!
Three-minute Emperors! It makes me want to kill,
to *kill.* Isn't that something? It makes me understand
revenge because I want to kill. Oh, Englishman, look
at me, I cry instead.

ACT TWO SCENE THREE

> *JANIKA and RAPHAEL are both cleaning down
> different sides of the same door. Rubbing, squeezing
> out cloth into pail.*

JANIKA Oh, it's not interesting. Boring old blue-stocking
stuff. We all have complaints. But endless long
monologues of complaint become a habit. I
deal with a woman in my social work who
complains – endlessly. Every day brings a calamity.
Her husband left her because she was full of long

monologues of complaint. She'd recite them – like the Ancient Mariner – grabbing at whoever was passing by in her life, sometimes forgetting she was passing some people for the second time and telling them again. I have many clients like that – they're not with you. They don't look at you. They just look at this awful vision of their life – one long monologue of complaint.

Oh, the suffering is real enough for them but it's draining for everyone else. And insulting, really, because the monologues are saying '*you* don't suffer what I'm suffering, *you* don't understand what I understand'. As though it's happening only to them, they've been singled out. And they make people around them feel guilty for any little bit of happiness they've managed to snatch from life. And friends leave them; retreat to protect themselves. Who wants to be reproached all the time? So, no long monologues of complaint. I don't want to drive *my* friends away. I need them.

From *The Rocking Horse* (a play for radio in 17 scenes)

Synopsis

Three people – two women, one black boy – on a bus in Brighton become fascinated by a brightly-coloured rocking horse they see in a window of a house. One woman is a retired pharmacist, the other is a lecturer in philology; the boy is having a hard time passing his A levels. The two women take him under their wing to help him pass his exams. All three are very curious about the story behind the rocking horse. The play explores the life of the couple who own the house – their son was killed in a traffic accident. The wife thinks her husband has grieved too long. He finally realises she's right. All five lives are brought together by the rocking horse in the window.

SCENE TWO, THREE VOICES – INTERNAL DIALOGUES

FIRST VOICE

CLARA   You're still lonely, Clara. You've created rituals for yourself but you're still lonely.

I sit here in my garden, Clara's garden, and I realise how much I love life, but it doesn't stop me feeling lonely, just lonely, lonely. Look at those colours, shapes, textures. Feel the cool evening air. So many lovely objects surround me, each a special memory. I watch the orchids from last year, day by day, wondering if a second growth will appear. It excites me. And my ankles aren't swollen, my eyesight's not bad, my hearing's okay, I can still walk without a stick, and thank God I don't need medication for anything. I would just like to kiss someone goodnight and wake up saying 'Good morning'.

'Make friends!' say my friends. Easier said than done. Younger women are scared of you because they see themselves in a few years' time, and older women are too desperate. You may be lonely, Clara, but you're not desperate. You still have appetites for living, just no one to share them with, no familiar body around the place.

On the other hand Jack's been dead so long I don't know that I could stand another body around the place. But to kiss someone goodnight and wake up saying 'Good morning'…

SECOND VOICE

AGNES I'm Agnes and I shall never forget. It will remain with me always.

We were in a restaurant. Very expensive. He wanted to buy me a special meal for a 'special occasion' he said. We were at the coffee stage. He drank his little espresso, held the cup in the air for a split second, laid it back in the saucer with a harshness I don't think he intended. I think he intended resolve. And he said: 'I'm leaving you, Agnes. I've fallen in love with another woman. The bill is paid. Goodbye.' And he stood up and left.

It came from nowhere, nowhere that I could identify anyway, so I was too shocked to say anything. My gaze just followed him to the door as he went through it, and I even thought, absurdly, that it was a joke and that he'd gone through the door to pick up something, like a surprise gift, and he'd soon reappear with his gorgeous grin on his face. But he didn't return and I just sat there with a deep blush on my face hoping no other customer had heard and that my blush had not been noticed.

The waiter approached and handed me an envelope. My hands were shaking and I dropped it into the coffee – mine was a regular, so it was a coffee-stained note I read which added to the shabbiness of the moment.

'Dear Agnes. It had to be like this, swift and sharp with no lead up of wretchedness, and in

a public place with no chance of an outburst.
You will find the settlement will be generous. It
had been wonderful and then it had not been
wonderful. It's no consolation now but broken
hearts mend. Paul.'

I could feel my throat filling with fury.

I knocked over a chair as I fled, and only when I was
sitting in a taxi did I realise I'd fled with the sound of
fury coming out of me.

He was wrong, the broken heart doesn't mend. You
put it together like a precious, broken cup that never
looks right, that looks wonky, that looks like what it
is: a broken cup stuck together with glue. You feel
as though if you pick it up the tea will run the other
way. You can never quite trust it to function as it
once did.

THIRD VOICE

RAMBO   Yeah! My family actually did christen me Rambo.
        Don't much look like him though. Don't think
        I much *want* to look like him, either. All them
        muscles – too heavy to carry around, man. Don't
        look much like anyone, in fact.

            Rap tapping sound as though on a chair.

                Try looking for me
                But I'm not there
                I'm a hole in di wall
                I'm not anywhere
                Di other guys
                Des easy to see
                Des just overflowing
                Wid personality.
                I look to di left
                I look to di right
                But I've disappeared
                Right outta sight

Bom diddy bom diddy
Bom bom bom
I used dem words
To fill a gap
I'm gonna cool it now
'Cos I hate rap
I hate rap
I hate rap
'Cos rap is a trap
Is a trap
For a sap.

Drumming stops.

Everyone thinks I should love rap 'cos I'm black.
Don't! Can't help it. Wish I could. It ain't easy hating
rap when you're black. Lose your friends. Puts you
on the outside. In the cold. Cold and lonely in the
cold outside. Can't help it. Wish I could. Hate rap
and you lose friends. Need friends.

Pause.

Where you going in your life, Rambo? Who knows,
Rambo. I'd like to get me a horse and go galloping
the world. How you gonna get you a horse, Rambo?
You gotta work, man, to get that horse. Horses don't
grow on trees, you know. Work, Rambo, work.
When you finished school you gotta work to get you
a horse. To get you *any*thing you gotta work.

SCENE THREE

MARVIN My son was killed here. Just there, where Cazenove
Road meets the Upper Clapton Road. He was
walking up this road when a crazy kid, who'd stolen
a car, swerved from the main road too fast. Couldn't
turn sharply enough. Mounted the pavement where
my son was walking, shuffling his feet in the autumn
leaves. He enjoyed the sound of crunching through
autumn leaves. Smashed into him. Didn't stand a
chance.

But I don't come just to visit the spot and lay flowers.
No, I come to walk the road and look at everything
he might have looked at for the last time. I think
to myself – he saw this before he died, and that.
Perhaps he was looking at that chestnut tree on the
left, full of leaves in the spring, and conkers in the
autumn. The kids would pierce a length of string
through a conker with a knot at the end so that they
could swing it without the conker coming off. And
they'd challenge other boys to a conker match. My
boy, his name was Jonty, Jonty discovered that if you
soaked a conker in vinegar it became quite vicious.

Look, here, the car smashed into him here. Just as
he was about to turn left and catch the bus to Manor
House underground station, home to Swiss Cottage.
It's a long road, Cazenove Road, and I walk it from
the corner of Alkham Road where he went once
a week to practise singing in a choir, right up to
here – where he sang no more.

I look at everything he might have looked at for
the last time. That old house there with its grey
stone and carved Victorian emblems. He loved the
architectural conceits builders decorated even the
poorest houses with, the gargoyles, the fruit, the
writhing boughs and curled leaves. And those street
lamps. He saw those. And these apartment blocks
set back from the road. Their names. He delighted
in the variety of street names and buildings. He saw
all these things up till here. And here, a step away,
he saw no more. Everything from this point on he
missed.

Here – he was alive, vibrant, curious;
beyond – nothing, blackness. Stand
here – everything to live for. A couple of steps
forward – emptiness. A life finished. Smash! Just
like that. (*Weeping.*) A precious life. Just like that. My
boy's one and only precious life. Just like that.

SCENE TWELVE

> *RAMBO is reading to AGNES an essay she has set him.*

RAMBO 'So there I was riding this horse galloping fast just hanging on to its neck. And she let me. She let me hang on there. She trusted me. We was comfortable together, like we'd always known one another. Galloping! Galloping! But it wasn't like galloping, it was like flying. Her feet didn't seem to touch the ground. We was a couple. "Go on," I whispered in her ear, "go on, fly me, lovely." She liked my voice, I could feel it. "I'm flying," she said. She talked back to me. "I'm flying. For you I'm flying." And I could swear that if only I'd known how, if only I'd known the secret, she would have been. If I'd known the right words or the right way to twist her head or pull her mane or grip her belly with my legs she really would have flown for me, galloping on air, up into that starry sky, all the way to the moon.'

SCENE THIRTEEN

MARVIN 'And there is nothing new under the sun!' says Ecclesiastes who was wrong, wrong, wrong – the morbid old bugger. As I was wrong. Wrong, wrong, wrong! Everyone should be allowed to reinvent the wheel. I even think we were born to reinvent the wheel. To build as though there'd been no cathedrals; write poetry as though there'd been no Milton, plays as though no Shakespeare, compose as though no Handel, paint as though Turner had never held a brush…

I tell you, 'And there is nothing new under the sun' is a wail, a moan. It cautions foolhardiness at the expense of astonishment. What! come upon the Grand Canyon and not be astonished because others have been astonished before you? Not be awed by learning just because since Gutenberg a million young scholars had steeped themselves in learning before you?

I tell you – everything is new under the sun to those who confront it for the first time. Like love. No lover thinks his love is stale because Romeo once poured out his heart to Juliet. Nor should he. To deny lovers the delight of discovering love as though they were the first lovers in existence is to shroud them in a mean spirit that would blight them for life. That festival of kites in Dieppe, that gondola in Venice, that Palio race in Siena – we were the first ones ever to see them all. They happened specially for us.

What I say is – let *every*one reinvent the wheel; let nothing be known under the sun. Nothing!

By the Same Author

Plays

THE WESKER TRILOGY: Chicken Soup with Barley; Roots; I'm Talking About Jerusalem

The Kitchen

The Four Seasons

Their Very Own and Golden City

Chips with Everything

The Friends

The Old Ones

Love Letters on Blue Paper

The Journalists

The Wedding Feast

Shylock

One More Ride on the Merry-Go-Round

Caritas

When God Wanted a Son

Lady Othello

Bluey

Badenheim 1939

Shoeshine and Little Old Lady (*Plays for young people.*)

Beorhtel's Hill

Men Die Women Survive

Blood Libel

Wild Spring

Break My Heart

Barabbas (*15 minute play for TV/stage*)

Denial

Groupie

Longitude

Letter to Myself (*For a 13 year old actress*)

Amazed & Surprised (*15 minute radio/stage play*)

Phoenix Phoenix Burning Bright

The Rocking Horse (*For radio*)

Short Stories

Six Sundays in January

Love Letters on Blue Paper

Said the Old Man to the Young Man

The King's Daughters

Essays and Non-fiction

Fears of Fragmentation

Distinctions

Say Goodbye, You May Never See Them Again
(Wesker text, primitive paintings by John Allin)

Journey Into Journalism

As Much As I Dare (autobiography)

The Birth of Shylock and the Death of Zero Mostel
(Diary)

For Children

Fatlips

When I Was Your Age

Novels

Honey

Opera Librettos

Caritas

Grief

Poetry

All Things Tire Of Themselves – a collection of 45
poems.